When *God* Called on my *Cellphone*

When God Called on my Cellphone

Robert Vincent Piro

To order additional copies of this book, contact:
Xlibris Corporation
1-888-795-4274
www.Xlibris.com
Orders@Xlibris.com
98729

Contents

DEDICATION

To Jesus Christ. It is my weakness that reveals strength; because of this weakness, I took and take in strength through Christ. If it was not for God's forgiveness of me, I could have never forgiven myself.

In God's grace I was freed.

Bowling in a sauna
Maddening heights in awesome sobriety
Lightning flashes of anger and lashing tongue whips against
metal doors
Papers flying of a tossed salad of what was thought to be
forgotten emotion
Shooting out the sky, the sky crashing into my
mountain—molten, exploding
Time broken into frozen frames, framing me in eternity
A character mad who just forgot how to scream, and his
screaming an emptying
A dash of spice into this overcooked food, and now I eat what
remains in a chilled spring day.

Some June day in 2008 I pulled into the driveway of the center. It was once originally—who knows? Something Catholic—a retreat or hostel. There were still some old nuns living there, but now it was a rehab. A rehab I had blown off a few weeks earlier. I call this place "Nonsensenon."

I was in my jeep with my angel dog—German shepherd "Shadow"—and I had returned to get my books. I paid $250 for those fucking books; whether they were full of shit, or not, I wanted them.

Next to the front of the building, this place was actually several buildings backing onto huge ancient-looking pine trees. Set up like a compound, there were three tiers of steps leading up to a huge stone altar. On top of the altar was a real-size Jesus in white crucified to a black metal cross. Good old brother Jesus frozen in metal worship. Just before driving off, I stopped and clicked a picture with my cell phone, and away Jesus went to rest in my cellular picture archives.

A month later, I am sitting in the driver's seat of my jeep, pipe in left hand, and I am nervously loading my pipe with crack for the first time in almost four months. My stomach is knotted. Forget butterflies; I have dragonflies bouncing off my inner abdomen, hitting the inside of my ribs. My heart is racing. Crack melted, pulling in the devil's cream, and *buzz, buzz, buzz*—my cell phone is vibrating on the front passenger seat. "What the fuck?" Who the fuck? I'm thinking. What timing. I open my cell, and there is Brother Jesus's photo out of my archives staring back at me. "Fuck." I close the phone, and I turn its power off. And now I am back on purpose.

On purpose—pipe in mouth and one hand holding it while my right hand flicks the lighter. Perfectly aiming the tip of the flame just below the edge of my pipe and *buzz, buzz, buzz*, the cell phone has turned on by itself. "What the fuck? Who the hell? It's fucking Jesus again!"

I put the pipe down, dropped my light, grasped the cell phone in both hands, and I snapped that fucking phone in half and began my three-month journey back into misery.

It was the only time ever God called me on my cell phone. What timing. He would have to wait till I was at least done with my crack and had finished coming down.

It is the late nineteen nineties. I am in Hamilton downtown, a few blocks just east of James Street on King Street itself, above a bar. This apartment building I have found myself in is not of the same world that is just outside its door. First stop in addiction is dark death and stinky dog shit. A prostitute who sucks cock while eating a chocolate bar, the candy bar and her pipe both still in her hands—this is a careful balancing act on one's knees. The apartment is on the second floor, a loft with windows facing the busy downtown King Street.

She wants me to go in her place first; she is terrified thinking there is someone in there waiting for her. I step in the apartment, and I am overwhelmed with the smell of rotting garbage and shit. Dog shit is everywhere, every few feet. A dog barking shut in the washroom. Amongst the shit on the floor there are clothes and garbage, food wrappers scattered everywhere. There are no lights and I find no one waiting, except now I have to check the second-story loft part. I climb the stair loft and peer into the darkness of more dirty clothes and a soiled single mattress with no sheets or blankets. I tell her all is clear, and this once-cute brunette white girl with beaded dreads walks in reluctantly.

She approaches me and begins whispering crazily into my ear. Seems this morning she went to check on her girlfriend who lives in the apartment next door and found no one except her friend's dead body on the bed. "He took her eyes," she says to me. Really, it is that after so many days of being dead our eyes sink into our skull; they only seem missing. She thinks she knows who killed her friend and, even worse, thinks he knows she knows. Long story short, she pulls out her pipe and does a toke of crack. I am at the window staring at the people walking on the sidewalk, thinking how oblivious they are. Or maybe they don't care. She is standing in the middle of the room, touching the back of her head; she begins jumping up and down in the spot she is standing in a panic. "Touch my head right here," she asks me. "No, here." I am thinking maybe she has fleas, but what she is really trying to say is that she thinks her head is on fire. "Are you sure I am not burning? I can smell smoke. Is my hair burning?"

She does another toke and rushes to the washroom. A little dog comes running out and begins scavenging the floor, sniffing his shit and the food wrappers. I am in what once may have been a kitchen, trying to find something to put water in for the dog to drink. She is in the washroom in darkness, now screaming at me to come help her, that her head or hair or some part of her is on fire. It's her brain that is fried. She is totally mad—too much drugs and malnourished with too little sleep for who knows how long. Today she responds to one name. Next time I meet her she will be someone completely different: different name, probably a wig on, and a totally different person with just the same anguished soul.

Welcome to my old reality; this is me at this time still a remnant of a successful person. I would be Rob in the hood and then later be named Black Rob. It is years before my dog has even been born, and little did I know that this nastiness would become my world for the next decade to come.

Do you know?
Have you ever
had to tell your people they were to die?
Hold them as they go,
bury them,
and then return to lose the war.

Image fades with time; it is my purpose that holds me forever sure in eternity. I am my purpose, my purpose is me. My image is nothing. When on drugs, I was a withering animal less graceful than a dog or alley cat, less deserving than a mouse in the field. In my sobriety, purpose found me and delivered me from myself and brought me to a place next to God himself with the angels.

In the front seat of my corolla. It is winter. The car is off. I am sleeping.

There is a knocking at my car door. I am so tired; beyond tired. I guess this is close to death. I am trying to wake, but I can't. There is just pain, splitting in my mind like it is in two.

My eyes open. I make my body move. "Yes," I answer the blue-uniformed officer at the door of my car.

Too tired to move, too tired to know I am awake. Just me and my pipe sleeping. *Bang-bang* through the window of my car. A lady's face with a police hat, a shimmer of a badge in the cold night. Then questions, questions that I cannot answer.

All I know, all I can say is what my name is. The rest is frozen in my mind, frozen in fatigue and cold. The splitting pain.

"Officer," I say, "take me to the hospital. I have a splitting pain in my head, I can't remember anything."

"Oh you're okay," she answers, "you just smoked too much crack. What street are you on?"
I cannot answer.
"What are you doing here?"
I cannot answer.
"Where are you coming from?"
I cannot answer.
"Are you going somewhere?"
I cannot answer.
"What day is it?"
I cannot answer.
"Where are you?" I cannot answer.

"Please, officer, take me to the hospital."
Her response: "Get out of the car."
The car door opens. *Clink*, my pipe hit's the frozen pavement.
"Sir, you're under arrest."

I had been with "J" and he was supposedly helping me turn four grams of crack, of which I owed money still for a half ounce, back into enough to pay back my dealer. But it just seemed he was stretching out his own high. Be careful when you fall because there are always those waiting to catch you just before you hit the ground. So to take anything you might still have then let you finish dropping to the ground hard. With just a few tokes left, one of my other dealers, Dan, and I all tisic on the phone with him, and screaming he says, "Black Rob, don't ever call my cell phone again." I do not even remember the last toke I did. For all I know, J could have butted me over the head with his gun and smoked it himself, or that toke could still be there, forgotten and melted on the pipe still years later in the sewer grade at Sherman and Main Street in Hamilton.

But the war is not over, and it is a good thing that the good are still putting up a good fight. I was just shell shocked, or should we say drug shocked, out of the battle. But in pursuit of the devil, I found a new front line, and I am fighting again among family and friends. The good fight against an evil encroachment on man. This evil is not of man but does or can dwell in him.

I am outside my vehicle. It is beyond cold. I feel as if my bones are bare against the night, against the cold of this cunt cop's car. My being against her car and the officer's being touching me allover, searching the nothing I have.

"If I find you back in your vehicle tonight, you're going to jail." She hands me a promise to appear because of the pipe. I guess the jail is full again, so I just get a court date for the possession charge. I don't care about any of this. I am just wondering how the hell I am going to get anywhere. I am too tired to even walk. I start moving my body slowly away from my car, away from the cop, toward warmth: a 7-Eleven store just two short city blocks away.

After being awake for almost nine days and nights with no sleep, what is being alive and what is being dead seem to blend into one. Not dead. Not alive. Not me. No, I was somewhere else.

Dreaming the past—yours not mine.
But I am now there as eyes seeing presently what is not.
A simple reminder—a voice on a phone, a ride in a car—
to places been but not seen,
faces known but not met.

The middle of the night, my jeep rolls silently to a stop on an exit ramp off the 40 East, about twenty kilometers before Trois-Rivieres, Quebec. I am out of gas. Anticipating the cold and its approach, I quickly close up all the windows of the jeep and jump in the backseat to cuddle as close as possible with my dog "Shadow." No one stops as they drive by; I don't expect anyone to stop either. In the past, I have nearly been killed trying to stop a car on the highway. Waving my arms like mad, even standing in the lane—cars just honked and dodged my body. It is miles and miles to the nearest phone. If not for the warmth of Shadow, I would probably have frozen; not just this time but countless others. This dog has kept me, a fucking addict who should have been dead many times over, alive. If not for this four-pawed German shepherd friend . . .

I sleep till the morning light in Shadow's warmth; morning commute drivers are much more likely to stop. Yes, in Quebec; forget about it in Southern Ontario. Some nice man stops. He drops me at the closest gas station; he even gives me five dollars for some gas. I run back to my jeep with my jerry-can of gas; Shadow and I get back to our apartment in Trois-Rivieres.

This highway, the 40, holds countless times we have been stuck—mostly when out of gas, sometimes just pulled over. Most memorable was when my dog Shadow, a working girl from Montreal, and one of my dealers, "Superman," were heading to Trois-Rivieres from Montreal. Superman is driving; he is a tall, bulky Italian with thick glasses and long hair. In the front seat beside him was a mulatto working girl; I can't remember her name. I am in the backseat. We are in a minivan; Shadow is sprawled out behind my seat. Superman was giving me and Shadow a ride. A day earlier, we had been pulled over in our jeep, and the police had impounded our vehicle for me driving a good 169 kilometers in a 100 zone. Oops.

Stopped on the shoulder of the 40, cruiser behind us with lights flashing, Superman is not getting out his license and registration; instead, he is loading as much of his crack as possible onto his stem. He hits it with his torch; it seems like minutes are going by as he is pulling on his stem. As he is toking away, I can see the officer approaching the side of the vehicle. Superman puts his stem down and rolls down his window for the officer as he is still exhaling clouds and clouds of smoke, beginning his conversation with the police officer in French.

Superman and the cop talk a bit, then the cop goes back to his cruiser. As the cop sits in his cruiser, Superman and the girl are smoking as much of their crack as quickly as possible. Again, I warn them of the officer's approach, and again, Superman is exhaling, this time just about right into the cop's face. I can hear the officer speaking in French, and it's like his speech is speeding up double time, his voice changing. He keeps going back and forth to his cruiser, then suddenly appears and apparently is letting us go without even a ticket. I guess these police don't know the smell of crack; I think he is actually stoned and does not know it.

We reach my destination, but with no dope as Superman smoked it all during his interrogation with the police officer. So if ever you get pulled over on the 40 East, just exhale a big puff of crack in the officer's face. You would be surprised; I was. Maybe they will let you go; odds are they won't even know what the fuck happened.

Closed in a room,
locked against hands
through the wood.
There are restless screaming tongues
and mad searching hands
crossing eyes more dangerous than bullets.
Teeth that could tear souls.

So, locked and barricaded, we are in a crack house, top floor in the most rear of the house. The room is not large, just a bed and two chairs with a small table in between by a little window we can barely fit through. A nasty ho named Wigs lives on the bed. I have never seen her leave this mattress on the ground. All she ever does is flick her lighters keeping candles going and lighting her pipe, crouching and crawling around the room; I don't ever even recall her standing. The door from the room to the rest of the house has a long wooden board against it going straight across the room wedged into the far wall.

It would probably be easier to come through the wall than knock that door down. The door itself has two small holes—sometimes you can see mad eyeballs from the other side—but through this hole money is received, and the crack goes out to the hall through the other hole. The small window is our way in and out of the house, and to get through, you must pull yourself up from the top of the second floor balcony below. If you are not expected, you may easily be pushed to a twenty-foot drop; but if you get in this room, you have entered crack heaven.

This is the Python house. Three brothers rent downstairs: one in jail for murder, one dying from some sort of disease, and the third, his twin, could also be Santa's twin, but on a crack diet with red hair. So this house makes money, but it is all small ten- and twenty-dollar sales. If a dealer enters this house from its front door, the cops are called from someone in the top room. Only those who feed Wigs dope can sell in this house; otherwise, the cops are on the way. It is like the cops work for the crackhead ho; they just don't know fuck-all.

Sometimes the door from the room to the wall starts to shake. The banging sometimes gets beyond deafening—tongues and eyes and fingers coming through the cracks in the wall and the holes in the door. So we stuff the holes with all sorts of dirty old shirts when no money is in the house. The last time I was in this house, I noticed from the other side that some had started trying to dig through the washroom wall in the back bedroom. Like I said, that room is crack heaven till one day that door or wall finally breaks—then good luck as the demons charge, bringing the retribution of God himself. It will be a quick jump out that small window two stories down, which would be nothing compared to being torn apart by crack dog-fiends.

And on this farm she had some daughters . . .

On crack in Hamilton is a dry desert place. The city is polarized. Crackheads and dealers and taxpaying citizens: where did all those acid potheads go from the nineties? Crack is everywhere in the city from east to west, north to south, on the mountain escarpment and off—and in the country, country farm crack houses. Yes, out in the distant country resided the Evil Lady. What a web that was—poor Johns caught in it, stuck to all that crack and porn.

It's a country house parked in the drive, a camper. I cannot bring Shadow inside because he does not take well to other dogs, and she has one. Shadow stays in my car, sometimes in the garage. In her kitchen, there are two fridges packed with food—all lifted, stolen from local supermarkets. The living room has a 1980ish feel to it, with family pictures strewn across the walls of her girls when they were young. Now her girls work. Grown up, they are paid to keep company with gentlemen for sex or just keep them jonesing while they smoke dope. In return, the Evil Lady receives payment from the men; all to keep this crack barn running smoothly with hot dogs and ice cream in the freezer. And yes, we cannot forget crack for the family. When things are rolling good, the agency advertisement makes the paper and all seems well, but when things slip up and customers have been reduced to empty pockets but don't leave and bad schemes go in place, the usual result is chaos. Men paying for sex from the girls also buy their tokes from the mother, and yes, sometimes Mom does a special combo with the one or both of the daughters for a special incestuous price. I have seen them rolling good and seen them sucking cock for twenty-dollar pieces of crack.

I park my vehicle beside the camper in the driveway, walk to the front door, ring the bell, and nonchalantly, just like regular Saturday-afternoon company, I am greeted by stepdad, offered a beer, and shown to the living room couch.

I was not there to get with a girl. I had met one of the daughters before; she had invited me to visit as a quiet place to smoke. Boy! Quiet was an understatement. Apparently, an ambulance had just left with some dead "John." This guy visited to get laid and was also put on the pipe. After three days of not taking whatever medication he was supposed to, some internal part of him stopped working. And now it seems this couch I am sitting on was just where the poor motherfucker just died. "So when is that dealer getting here anyways?" I ask.

I spend days hanging out with the daughters, smoking dope while one of them is rotated out for calls. Occasionally the mother takes one of the daughters and goes to sit in one of the client's houses; slowly, the house is emptied of its belongings. Dealers treat the household as if it's an "on display" home shopping channel. By the time I am called to pick them up, I find the poor guy sitting in his empty living room, cross-legged on the floor. Even the drapes went for a resin toke. On the kitchen counter, a broken framed plaque—some rehab graduation thing. Shit, I think, I got to remember the name of that rehab, Nonsensenon, so I am careful never to go there. Apparently, this guy relapsed on his doorstep when he just returned from rehab, did not even make it through his front door: home not even for a second yet and back on the pipe.

Fast-forward. It is a year later. I am graduating a rehab program. I receive my framed certificate. I look at it and remember that font and color, and now the name is familiar. Nonsensenon. A look of shock inside me—it's identical to the one I found a year ago smashed on that poor guy's kitchen counter. Shit! I think, I came to the wrong place. He lasted not even a minute. But not me; no sir. I last five days sober, then it's back to the crack.

The Evil Lady orchestrated hooking her clients for sex on to dope through her working-girl daughters, and selling crack, she maintained her high and dominance in her family. A truly evil bitch indeed.

She would say to me, "It's good to keep an apple with you. If a cruiser ever pulls up beside you at a stop light when you're high, you pull out your apple and have a bite."

Was that what she was doing when she slammed her camper into a stopped vehicle on the highway on ramp, killing the other driver? No, she was nodding for lack of dope. I wonder if, while waiting for one of her daughters to come out from a call, did she have a bite of her apple? While waiting for her daughters to finish sucking cock. If ever low on dope, had to keep company with her apple, and if so, did she bring two apples that night, or did the crackhead whore mother, daughter-pimping cunt have to drive back to that country crack house all alone with her prostitute daughter without an apple? It was never her doing, she thought. She felt she never had a choice in any of all this; she was just an addict too.

Wheels

I have been camped out at the Evil Lady's house for weeks, and my buddy "Wheels" has locked himself in the washroom. All I can hear is his screaming. Wheels is a skinny crackhead who we call by this name because for some time he was reduced to movement in a wheelchair. He was a victim of a home invasion years ago, awoken in bed and stabbed several times, suffering loss of movement in his legs. I first met Wheels at the old Holiday Inn Hotel on King Street in Hamilton. After introducing himself, he introduced me to his wife, a metal pipe for crack. He told me his pipe was his wife. I would not understand this till my own addiction reached a zenith of itself, then I realized the only thing important as crack was one's pipe. One's pipe needed to be guarded, cared for, and cherished as if it was the only thing that mattered. Wheels is now locked in this dirty, dingy, stinking well-water washroom, trying to have a bowel movement. He is self-administering himself enemas—first with shampoo bottles, but now with a garden hose I have run into the house for him from outside.

This all started days ago when he asked me for some dope and said that he would pay me back later, explaining he had hooped—stuffed a bunch of crack and tobacco up his asshole. Apparently, there was a warrant out for Wheels's arrest, and knowing this, his plan was to turn himself in while holding massive amounts of crack and tobacco in his rectum. Once in jail, he would poop it out and make a lavish amount of money and enjoy a comfortable stay in jail. Problem was, each day when it came time to drive Wheels down to the police station, he would get cold feet and not leave the car. Now it has been over a week, and he has not shit. He was telling me he was having stomach cramps. I told him that if he doesn't shit soon, he is going to have to go to the emergency. Imagine explaining this to the surgeon after he just removed a ball of crack and bail of tobacco from your solidified anus. I have given him no option and have told him to either shit or go to the hospital. Last thing I need is my buddy's intestine exploding while I am doing a toke.

His screaming has turned from short spasms to sudden prolonged wails. It seems we have movement. I kick in the washroom door and begin taking pictures with my cell phone of a squirming Wheels sitting on the toilet. Pants around his skinny legs, this orange-bearded man with crazy blue eyes screams at me. "You bastard!" There is nothing he can do to stop me. The shit has begun to roll out, and he is now screaming in relief, both his hands pressed against the toilet seat underneath his butt. He finishes and falls of the toilet and begins crawling away. I turn my cell phone to the toilet and see what I never thought possible. There in the bowl is what must be an eighteen-inch-long shit spotted throughout with orange plastic. He has hooped not just drugs, but the skinny mad bastard had actually shoved full plastic-wrapped cigarettes in himself with weed and crack. Wheels now has his pants on and, after doing a toke, crawls back to the toilet on hands and knees to salvage his next toke out of his shit. I am texting my new pictures to every number on my phone.

Never Made It to the Falls

B ack when you can say I was a functional drug addict and alcoholic, I had lots of party friends. All the best of friends when double fisted at the bar and you had desk drawers full of weed and a glove box in the beamer 7 series with a big bag of cocaine.

Our usual spot on Hess Street in Hamilton was a loose bar where I would drink till I puked right at the bar, then the bartender would just drop newspapers on the ground near where I was and all would continue festively. Way back in the day, the nights would start here and, the next morning or afternoon, it would end in some dingy crack apartment somewhere. Usually, by then it would be me alone, just a pounding headache of the sobriety I dreaded to return to.

One night the plan was to hit Niagara falls, but after too many early evening drinks at the local spot, I asked our limo driver to pull over for a moment at the corner of King and Sherman. One of my buddies came in with me and the others were left waiting in the limo. At some point my buddy bailed on me, and I walked back out to the limo in the morning light. All of them were gone, kind of like a heads-up that I did not clue in on.

This was some apartment building, three levels, and I swear every tenant was a crackhead. If the door was open, it meant they were out of crack or waiting; if shut, they were smoking away, not to be disturbed. The halls echoed with odd noises and horrible reminders of what really was going on. I remember doing tokes and thinking I could hear people calling my name outside looking for me; it was like I was hearing my family call for me in my head. There was never anyone actually outside, and that sense would disappear with the next toke and be forgotten till I was alone without a buzz again. I eventually got banned from the building, not by the police or landlord but by the actual crackheads themselves who became terrified of me, especially when I would first show up drunk as hell. I remember one night, either myself or my buddy pulled the fire alarm. We were smoking away at our crack, and I peeked out the door and saw a fireman walking through the halls. No, man, the only fire here is my Bic hitting my pipe.

This building was fucked indeed. The resident dealer in the building had a girlfriend who he cut with a knife in her sleep for robbing him. She later took out her frustration on some chick who could not pay. She doused her with some sort of lighter fluid and set her on fire.

Such a building you cannot say I was lucky to walk out of, or in, with both money and myself still attached. Call it blessed; but why?

In an instance it is off,
something gone from all—
an entire world cleansed in one moment.
I am standing in awe,
wonder, amazement—freed
as now I easily be
that which I could not before.
This new being ended a sense of want—
want no longer attached to anything,
want no longer real.
Just me in my wonder and awe
at an already beautiful world.

I am in rehab; it is over ten years past since those good old party days. This is not my first rehab, but at least my fifth. Call me a professional at this now. I am in my dormitory room. I am happy, and I am clean.

Not all rehabs are like this one; in fact, I would say this one rehab is of its own kind. This rehab is Nonsensenon. It was not always easy to clean up, and some rehabs were horrific for me coming off dope. But I am here. I am happy. I am in my room. My room number is 38, and it is macked out! Big mini fridge full of cheese and prosciutto (I have it mailed in to me), a closet shelf full of Del Monte canned fruit, and of course, an espresso machine with a fifteen-pound stockpile of Real Italian espresso grind. Life is good. No complaints.

A young lad named Scudz enters my room. He used to be addicted to heroin but not anymore, and he came off the dope without the help of other drugs. Yes, that is right; and I have seen many others like him come off that opiate shit without other drugs to help, just people to help. Eventually though, very few decide for themselves to continue their life clean, but Scudz does.

He picks up a copy of my poetry book and is standing in the middle of my room reading it. As he is reading it, I am watching him. He is touching his dick through his pants, and he looks at me and says my room stinks.

"Stinks?" I say.
"Ya, like sausage," he says.
I point out to him my Italian cacciatore hanging from my window.

One thing rampant in rehabs is sex. My first rehab years ago consisted of a constant regular regime of blowjobs in the washroom. I am told by most in this rehab and others that relationships in rehab, even if only sexual, spell *relapse* later. Not like the girls here are much anything anyways. My first night in this rehab with Scudz, three guys are caught in the women's dormitory.

"Wow, these girls." Scudz laughs. He reminds me a lot of this guy Brad Janes; it's haunting. Scudz is a white boy—Russian heritage, shaved head.

"You remind me so much of Brad Janes," I tell him.

"Who's Brad Janes?" he asks.

"Brad Janes use to be head of discipline here at this rehab," I answer.

Scudz shoots back, "Get lost. I remember him, you mean I am that much of a dick? He was the most not-liked guy around here, pretty much everyone hated him."

I say, "He was good. At least I thought till I relapsed in Montreal and called him for a ride. But I can't tell you that story now, but I will one day. I have lemon-ginger tea that was mailed to me. I am going go make some and go stare at the fat chicks."

Scudz says, "I mean even if one of those chicks came in my room in the middle of the night standing there naked, not even then would I."

"Would what?" I ask.

This kid we call Elvis comes in my room at that moment; he wants to trade me a Players for a Dumaurier. I say to him, "Just take a smoke."

He answers, "But do I have your permission?"

They are all laughing because they see me writing down in my journal all this as it happens; they know I am going to write a book when I am done with this rehab.

Elvis takes his smoke and gives me a hug. Another guy enters my room—let's call him Carlton—a tall, long, languid fellow. "Black Rob, my sister is an actress. She needs a script."

I never do get a chance to tell Scudz that story, so I will tell it now.

When You Relapse: Who Not to Call

So I am meeting this guy, a discipline officer at Nonesensenon named Brad Janes. I am supposed to meet him at the McDonald's on Rue Forges. I have just got back in town, Trois-Rivieres, from Montreal. I Have relapsed after being four months clean. He was supposed to meet me, pay my ride, tuck me in back to bed, and drive me to drop my dog the next day and then me to rehab. He calls my cell phone and says he is coming to my place instead. I was trying to avoid this because I still have my ride from Montreal at my place, smoking crack, and Brad Janes himself used to smoke crack. And yes, I don't want to put him in danger. He shows up at my door with this chick Jewel, another one from the same rehab; she is a recruiter. They push their way into my place. I am standing in my kitchen talking to Brad Janes. I am fucked up, but all I notice is that this guy reeks of mouthwash, and I feel he is trying to distract me from Jewel. A moment later, Jewel appears in the kitchen. "Here," she says and hands me a bag of crack. "If it's your last night, you might as well have some fun. We will pick you up in the morning." My ride from Montreal leaves and so does Brad Janes and Jewel. I see all their cars together shoot down my road caravan style. I close my eyes and see them all meeting at the corner store, Brad Janes and Jewel buying all the crack the ride had. No, I think, that can't happen. I shake my head and busy myself with my crack till morning comes.

How much not of a surprise when my ride to rehab appears at my door in the morning. Not just him but also Jewel and—again, no big surprise—yes, also my dealer from Montreal and his girlfriend as well. It's a morning smorgasbord; it's oeuffs a la crack ce matin.

"It seems there is just a little change in our plans," Brad Janes says to me. I look at him in front of me, fidgeting with a crack stem he has pulled out of his pocket.

In the most serious tone I can muster, I say to him words that in the past I have always found are a foolproof plan when events seem to be out of control, "Let's get a room."

After an hour's ride into Montreal behind my dealer's car and a quick stop at Western Union and then at my dealer's house, Brad Janes, Jewel, and myself are in a hotel suite smoking our brains out with crack. Shadow is in Jewel's car. The whole time while smoking, Brad has one eye out the peephole of the room, his body wedged over the door and his other eye on his pipe. It would have been physically impossible to enter our room through the door with that sweating motherfucker stuck like that between it and the wall—stem in one hand, cell phone in the other, eye glued to the door eyehole.

After smoking steadily for some hours, I bring up the topic of work to Brad. "So how are things at the rehab, how's the job?" Not a moment later, the fire alarm is going off in the room. Brad has exhaled a huge toke directly on the sensor. He begins panicking, beginning to run around the room then jerking his body back to a stop, back to the eyehole, then charging toward the washroom, then back to the peephole. Back and forth insanely for like a minute then *boom*, out the door he goes and slams the door behind. Jewel and I look at each other; we get the alarm off. I peek into the hallway out the door; Brad Janes is gone. We sit in the room a bit, wondering where the hell he went. I go outside and take Shadow for a walk. I cannot find the guy anywhere. Back in the room with Jewel, a couple hours go by and still no sign of the guy. I figure, if he was still running, he should be the near the dealer's house by now. Jewel and I jump in the vehicle to go check the dealer's house; maybe he went back there.

I leave Shadow again in Jewel's car, and Jewel parks in a spot around the corner from my dealer's house. In this little apartment off of Rue Hoocelaga in Montreal, smokers converge usually from my dealer's house to sit and smoke crack; rooms are rented by the hour in the rear for those who wish private time with working girls. I tell Jewel, "Whatever you do, don't take any dope from anyone, even if they say it's free. Nothing is really free here."

I run across to my dealer's spot, Chez B. Brad Janes is not there and has not been there. I get some dope quickly and return to Jewel. It's just taken me about twenty-five minutes and all the clunkers in the apartment are saying Jewel already owes over two hundred bucks; what a fuckin' fean bitch. I mean in less than thirty minutes she has been stripped of all her jewelry, fancy winter coat, and supposedly owes all this money. I tell her not to worry. All the dope in this spot comes from my dealer, and he and I are on good terms. She doesn't seem to be hearing what I say. I have no money, but I have good credit with the dealer so I am not worried, but I do ask her to drive me somewhere. One of the clunkers wants to come with us to make sure we don't take off. I am pulling Shadow out of the backseat so he can piss, the clunker standing by me on the curb, and Jewel hits the gas of her vehicle and takes off.

Shadow and I are left stranded in Montreal. We live in a town over a hundred kilometers away—some Friend. That's what you call a true rehab friend. You never really know them until you smoke crack with them. What is that saying, "I guess I didn't know her from Adam"? It is a cold February night, and the streets of Montreal are unkind when you have no money. Shelters close early; good luck trying to keep from freezing in the subway stations when you have a dog with you. Thankfully, Shadow and I have a big tab with this dealer, and we are accommodated till morning. It is the middle of the next night when Shadow and I get back to our little Quebec town of Trois-Rivieres. I pay Mr. Brad Janes a visit; he is warm and comfortably reclined on his couch with a rye-and-coke in hand.

"So you still want that ride to Ontario? If you do, that's fine. I have a few days of work. I just want you to get me some crack though, to start." Brad Janes slurs to me. Some fine discipline office this rehab has; they sure know how to spot potential winner employees. It's quite ironic, maybe more sad; in this same small apartment building, there are other staff living who work at the same rehab, and all this goes on just around the corner of the actual rehab center, right under their noises but also right in front of their eyes.

So it's another round-trip to Montreal via rehab discipline officer Janes himself, my dog Shadow, and I. This time we all return together to my apartment. I don't know how I am going to do this. I mean I am almost out of money, and this guy is out control, power smoking. I am trying to slow him down, but it's not working. I guess our departure to Ontario would have to wait till the morning when I had gotten more money. Janes does not seem to like this idea. He is in my bedroom alone. I have a working girl from Montreal staying in my place; she is cleaning. Janes's cell phone keeps getting texts. I am on my own phone making plans for the morning departure and the unthinkable happens. It seems that, with no crack, Janes has sold us out and has sent a text to his rehab bosses telling them that he is at my apartment. There is a banging on my door, and three individuals from the rehab where Janes works, where I had attended, are at my door. I open my door and tell them to leave, but they don't. The one woman, an executive—let's call her Chubby—is peeking through my front window. I open my front door, and we butt chests. I am infuriated that they won't leave my doorstep. I mean I do have neighbors. I go in my den and pick up a big thick book, some Ron Hubbard scientology book gifted to me by the rehab. I open the front door and fling it at the executive, slam the door, and yes, I call 911.

"Police, there are three people at my door and window. They keep banging my door, they won't leave." I am told by the police to ignore them, just pretend they are not there. When Janes hears me call the police, he finally appears from the bedroom and says it's his fault they are here and they are only here for him; he exits my place. I am watching from my door as they grab him and throw him into his car. I yell, "You're all a bunch of closet crackheads, poor excuse for a rehab!" One of them screams back at me, "Go fuck yourself!"

I am shaking and upset. I mean it was their staff who, instead of helping, used me to get more drugs, and when it comes down to it, I know there are other staff who are closet users. And me, a past client, is in the mess of this confusion. And it seems no matter what I try to do or who I reach out to, I can't get myself out of my situation. Now that all is in the open, it is apparently my fault that Brad Janes and Jewel relapsed. I am torn with guilt, but Jewel tells me after that the crack smoking with them did not start with me but months earlier, and it involved other staff who started bringing crack to her apartment. A few days later, I speak on the phone with the head of this rehab. He offers me to come back and redo part of the program; that's what I do. I also tell him another certain staff member is using besides Brad Janes; he responds that the person was not using drugs. He was wrong.

Total rehab stints for me are like seven times—five times at this one rehab. So you can say I have a bit of a history with this one particular Nonsensenon. They profess a success rate of 70 percent; that is more like their failure rate. But none of this changes the fact that a rehab is a place to clean up and that is the first most helpful step to getting clean. Just don't let them trick you and make you feel like you got this cured when you are not. Knowing the potential danger each day of returning to drugs is what I consider remaining humble, and knowing there is no security from addiction is itself the first security in overcoming it.

You can just keep going,
Sleep saving you once in a while.
But when the money runs out
And no one takes you in
When the tank goes dry
And the only possession is your teeth
There is nothing left
But to meet God and squeeze the sun
—from *A Place Called Wandering*

I am walking, no I am sleeping, no I am walking—walking away from my car and the cop and the cop's car parked behind my car. I step over the curb and onto the snow. I take a step, another step. I take a step. I am sleeping—no, awake again. A step, asleep, awake, a step, asleep, awake, a step. This goes on for like at least an hour, and I have moved around ten or fifteen feet. And I don't know; I forgot about the cop. I forgot about my car. All I know is the 7-eleven, the realest real to me, and I can see it, but only when my eyes are open. Each time I fall back to sleep, I slow to a pause and forget all, then I wake from losing balance, and then I see the store again and then that is all I know. But then I doze off again, and again it is a forgetting.

Hours later, I am sleeping peacefully in warmth until woken. "Get out, you can't sleep here. Leave!" I am being yelled at by a 7-Eleven attendant. I have been sleeping in an aisle on top of a pile of floor mats. Maybe if I ignore him and just fall back to sleep all will be well. No, not really.

"Just give my five minutes, mister."

He snarls at me. "Get out!"

I am trying to walk out of the store without falling back to sleep. Outside now, I rest against a payphone and begin dialing some number—who knows what number, but some number collect. Each time I begin dialing, I fall asleep before I can finish, and then within a few minutes, I am woken by a customer coming in or out of the store. I have no idea what time it is, what day it is, what month it is. Just ask me my name, that's all I can answer.

Not Every Day Is the Same

I remember the first days trying to be clean. I would go just a few hours into my day, and the cravings would start and they were severe. Each day, I would make it a bit farther through the day until those thoughts of getting high would begin. At the NA meetings they would say "one day at a time," meaning if you made it through one day, you could make it through every day. Each day was just another day to make it through. Unbeknownst to me, there were certain days when, without reason, I would suddenly let go and snap. That one night that would suddenly be different than the previous nights, when sleep is another far-off place, and all at once, you find yourself at your old dealer's door.

Those days were like practice walks for me; now I look at it like one life to live. I don't know if that is another saying of recovery. But that old life is not for me anymore. I still crave from time to time; sometimes it's as bad as being nauseous and not being able to move. When it gets like this, I pray away the feeling, let myself loose inside till I slip through and fall back into the comfort of what is, for me, Jesus. Suddenly, I am safe again. I know that even thinking or craving drugs is not all that bad, that I can see it as the temptation it is and know I can still refuse. I used to hope that the cravings would go away, and if I could just make it through till then. Now I accept the temptation; I don't wish it away. I carry it as a cross, just like we all have something to bear. I bear it, I carry it, I smile in it—because in all this wanting, it's the worst that can happen. Unless I use, and I know now that as long as I don't use, all is fine, even if that craving remains. It's like an arthritis or something like that. However hard it can get again, it's not the hardest it's been, and the more I persevere through it, the less it holds on to me.

Vigilante turned criminal,
man turned ape.
Once acting,
now pretending.
Once living,
now dead.

The first time I met "Sen," I had just been jacked by the police—pulled up and out of my Dodge Ram, the police going in to search my truck with my dog Shadow still in it at the time. My dog would have been done for if not for Sen running up to the cops. He told the cops he knew the dog and removed Shadow before they began their search. I was going in the back of a cruiser and did not care now knowing that someone I could later find had care of my dog and would watch him. I did not know him but knew his brother, who we called Crackman. I later met up with Sen in a crack apartment on Rebecca Street and got my dog back. I took care of Sen for helping me.

Sen used to not smoke crack. When his kid brother went out and started smoking crack and playing in the streets of Hamilton among crack houses and dealers, Sen followed. But Sen followed with his friends and baseball bats and went through wherever the younger brother went; they cleaned out crack houses and beat the dealers, flushing their dope, taking their cash. One day, who knows how, Sen started smoking the crack himself. Over the next few years, Sen went from a tough fighter to being a crack fiend with a limp in and out of Barton Street Jail. I last heard he was killed while trying to rob a dealer—stabbed to death. I am sure he was not intending to flush that dope but probably smash it with a needle.

So be it: one man entered a war and not only lost his life but his soul in the battle he waged. The means to truly effectively battle against any evil must be and only be love—otherwise, in the fight, you become the enemy yourself. Trickery of emotion, the devil's deceit.

Free From Drugs, But Not Free

I am in a private rehab in Trois-Rivieres, Quebec. Nonsensenon. In the course room of this rehab, very perplexed with the text book I am reading. The text is going on something like all the bad things that have happened to me were just a result of my previous bad actions. So I look up to my instructor and ask, what about kids born into war, babies being bombed out of their mother's arms? I mean, if I force myself to, I can see some links between losing family and my actions, but what about, for example, tragedy that happened to me as a baby? The instructor says he cannot answer that question, but maybe someone upstairs can.

I am sitting upstairs now in the office of one of the executives, the meeting happens as a result of me relapsing and having to return to this rehab. I am talking to her about all the bad things that happened to me as a child and a terrible reoccurring nightmare I used to have as a child. She asks me if I believe in reincarnation, and if so or not, was it okay to discuss the idea. She pulls out from behind her desk a thin but big book and begins showing me pages from it. It is about what they call engrams, a term from scientology, and the pictures are like those from a children's book, but this book is not for children. This book is like a beginner's introduction to scientology. The conversation, maybe all the bad shit in my life is the result of misdeeds I did in a previous life. So, does the answer to my addiction lie in scientologist ideas? I am raised Catholic, and how terrible it would be for me as a soul if recovery meant exchanging my religious beliefs. It would take me a couple years and even relapse again and again to choke this darkness out of my life, this attempt of darkening who I really was. A denial of my nature, a blaming onto my nature and a seemingly imperfect chance at recovery because I could not reconcile my true belief with this rehab's own religious teachings. Yes, I was naive. Yes, a victim.

When a person is dying of cancer, or a heart attack, they get to a hospital and don't ask the doctor too many questions per se. They are desperate; they are dying. So drug addiction is not too much of a different scenario. Someone faced with overdose or jail or extreme sickness from withdrawal, they don't have the liberty of asking what the rehab entails. Probably, they'll only ask if it works. Usually, neither does the family have such an opportunity either; they are desperate too. Time is of the essence to get a willing addict into rehab, and when you have a private rehab toting a fake success rate along with no waiting lists, it is too good to refuse.

Fortunately for people coming in unconscious into hospitals from car accidents or desperate with vital organs shutting down, in the lack of time and/or clarity to ask the doctor what they are doing, there are laws, regulations, and creeds to the profession that are in place. But with rehabs in the province of Quebec, there definitely does not seem to be such protection or professional standards set in place. I woke withdrawing to drugs being subjected a new system of belief, a way of living that was not compatible with my Christian upbringing. Either I would ignore and refuse it, block out those parts, or in my vulnerability, embrace it. Which I did; it only brought me back to the same relapse and place time and time again. I was trying to trade in my addiction for membership in a group that promised, in exchange, freedom from drugs. Even this promise was not true.

Now I don't want to knock anybody's beliefs, but if the medicine for my addiction was to be applied scientology minus the name, fine, but at least be truthful to the person about it. I mean, if I wanted, I could go stay with Zen monks to help in my living, or read Buddhist writings, which I do. But it's not like I am not aware of what the source is. Is this Quebec rehab like, or is it not like, taking one medicine labeled as another name? Or even worse, a placebo labeled as a medicine. I mean what is the cure or solution for an addict? Who knows, but at least, the rehab should be frank in saying what it is attempting. If not so, why? What does it, or why does it, need to hide its true identity? For a religious center to dress itself up as a secular one, plus with no medical doctor or nurse or any staff qualified by medical or social counseling standards, this is blatant fraudulent use of the word *rehab*.

Could I open up a rehab full of Catholic priests dressed in plain clothes and administer sacraments to ailing addicts, all just under different names and titles bearing no semblance to their true religious source, and worse, with no professional credibility or accountability as far as the truth in its success or failure? Apparently, I could if I wanted to in Quebec, as it is occurring today but with scientologists.

Two years later and I am working at this same rehab; on my day off, I miss a demonstration outside of it on the street. The next day at work, I am told by an executive that this was a demonstration by a hate group. This is also what is told to other employees and clients. It was said that the demonstrators were handing out pamphlets on how to kill yourself. In the next few weeks, through the internet, I am in contact with one of the demonstrators, someone whom I met at this center; we were both clients together. So I was lied to by the rehab about the nature and reason of this demonstration, even given a wrong name for the group by the executive. How could such a lie be justified? As if any lie could be justified. If this rehab was not doing anything wrong, what protection would dishonesty bring? All of sudden, this executive who was like a light to me does not seem any different than the rest of the crud of society. I am crushed, depressed over this, almost nauseous. Some fucking integrity.

How about this? Mr. and Mrs. Private Rehab, why don't you stick your lies in your ass sequence and see what you get? I mean it is us clients who lose everything when we fail to get clean; you don't even lose a statistic in your success rate because that's bullshit too. Not to say this rehab is all bad; there are some good points to the program, especially detoxification with the help of a sauna, and I have nothing against scientology. That is that I am really aware of it as just different beliefs. But I am against deceit. There are still many who work at this rehab who I do care about—some not a part of the lies—but yes, I still care about even some who participate in the dishonesty. But the question remains: why would anybody pretend to be different than who they really were, unless it was simply the truth being known that was feared? And if the truth is feared, how is that a starting point for getting clean or any sort of good living? What type of example is that?

A sudden flash,
and all is gone.
White, like a blank page.
A desert white, and in it only distant sounds of what once was
real,
and the only warmth is that of what was me escaping from my
body
through any and every possible pore in my skin.

I have been cooped up by my own choice for days and days in the Lance Motel at the highway corners. Partying with two chicks—a rental car, a 300, it is in the parking lot—and this whole party has gone from great to hopeless from high to highness impossible to maintain. Let's say in a few days, a few ounces of crack, lots of pot and whiskey, and I just took seven Viagras at once. But what is getting me the most high right now is the smell of this fucking chick's nail polish remover. What the fuck, man, I think, this is fucking brutal. I have had so much sex with the other one—let's call her the evil lady's daughter—that it feels like my ribs are busted; the other nail polish bitch just fucked up the coke with the last powder. I have to go into town to get more. No dealer will deliver; they all cut me off because they want me to sleep. I have only been awake for a week. "What's the big deal!" my friend Dan said to me. "Black Rob, whatever you do, do not come back in the city tonight." Oh well, what the dealer doesn't know won't hurt him.

I am in the rental 300 driving into the city; it feels like the driver's seat is angled facing the middle of the car's front. I try to straighten the seat, but the electric controls are not working. I have stabbing pains in my side. Did

I say *pain*? That is an understatement. I am driving down Main Street in Hamilton, and I am a good few minutes still from my destination. But I have to pull off the road; the pain is preventing me from breathing. I am in a Canadian Tire parking lot. I am not even pushing the gas of the car anymore; the 300 is just drifting. I slam the car into park, open the door, and pull myself out.

I am looking across the parking lot. In the distance, I can see balconies of an apartment building. Someone on a balcony is yelling to me; I cannot make out who it is or what he is saying. I begin walking from the vehicle. The pain, wow. I take a few more steps, and suddenly, a whiteness begins to spread everywhere. In less than a second, everything that was is gone. All I can see is a white emptiness; the only reality is a distant voice still shouting for my attention. I fall. I fall flat forward, the front of my face catching my fall on the cement. I cannot move. I am frozen; when I try to move, there is only pain everywhere in me. I am not even aware if I am still breathing. All I can sense around me is liquid, as if I am in a puddle. I am in a puddle. I fear it is blood—but how? An eternity passes, then I hear a voice. "Robbie, brother."

The voice belongs to Dalli, a Jamaican friend of mine. How he is there at that moment I do not know. I say to him, "Tell Dan I love him. In my pocket are my keys. Give them to Fats to give to my mother. Tell my mom to bring my dog back to the breeder. Tell Dan I love him. Tell Fats I forgive him."

I lay frozen in wet and pain.

I lay waiting to die.

I hear paramedics.

They try to turn me; I scream in pain. The world reemerges with vision again. I see the cement ground and see I am in a puddle of my own sweat. I am lifted onto a stretcher, into an ambulance. I lose consciousness.

I come to in an emergency hallway, fluids being pumped into me. A ministroke, I am told. And exhaustion. I am released the next day. I hobble out of the emergency in a ripped shirt looking for a payphone—a depleted body, a hurting soul with no answer to all the pain. I guess what the dealer doesn't know can hurt me.

And the soul aches
As it tries to wake
Fire into my mind
As I am tired of time
Of not hearing
Not seeing.

I am lying in a bed. I am woken by an older gray-haired lady; she is a nurse. "Oh you poor soul," she says to me, "I have to complete your intake." I fall back to sleep. I think some time passes. She asks me a question; as I begin answering her, I fall back to sleep. What should have been a twenty-minute intake interview takes more like a day and a half. I am in my first rehab. It is a four-week twelve-step program. Besides jail and when in the hospital, this is my first taste of sobriety in over fourteen years. Everything hurts, and I can barely walk.

This rehab is plush, with wide hallways and beautiful large washrooms, but the doctors here tell us that we are forever this way. That we have some extra or missing gene, something like that, and this will always make us addicts. The success rate of this rehab is said to be 3 percent, and we are told these are good odds. One of the guys I meet in this rehab kills himself a few days after finishing, found dead in his mother's washroom—the guilt of relapse. This place is huge; it is an actual hospital, a government rehab. There is one wing for drug addicts, one wing for sex addicts, another wing for people with eating disorders, and a fourth wing for trauma victims. Here, there are guys just coming back from the war in Afghanistan. In the evening, we are all permitted out front to smoke, but only till ten o'clock. We all mingle alike with our cigarettes. There is some old lady who walks amongst our crowd, asking for cigarettes; apparently, she is some victim of a lobotomy when young. Yes, this is the "Loonewood," and indeed, we are all loony. All of us can be compartmentalized into one wing or the other; I could probably qualify for each wing easy.

But in thirty-one days I feel good and begin what seems to be a full-time job of recovery. Discharged from the rehab, I go to three NA meetings a day—anywhere, any meeting I can find, and go for outpatient meetings two nights a week, and these meetings I don't like.

We are all seated in a circle of chairs, and for an hour and a half, I listen to how well everyone else is doing. I watch them gorge themselves with coffee, cake, and cookies.

After five meetings, it is my turn to speak. "My name is Black Rob, and I am an addict. My clean date is November 11 (it is now the first week of January). Although this is the longest I have ever been clean since an adolescent, I must say I feel horrible. There is not a single day I do not cry. I go to meetings, work out at a gym, work my steps, pray, go to church, spend time with my family, but must say I am in fear and sadness. I am sitting here listening to you all every meeting and am in indifference and hostility toward you all. I cannot identify with all your cheerfulness. I am in doubt how long I can hold on without using again."

The meeting is over; no time for any of them to comment. I get up and leave. That is the last of those meetings I ever go to. The next night, I am at an NA meeting at the YMCA in Hamilton. On break from the meeting, I tell some of the fellows that I have to go because I have my dog in the car. Jed looks at me. I feel he knows, and/or can see that I am about to go back out to use. "Just take care of yourself and be careful." His expression is deadening in sincerity and concern. I nod good-bye to him and walk away with the intention of betrayal. Betraying as I walk from this group of suffering clean addicts; this hurts. I still think of Jed sometimes today. I hope he is fine.

I am in my vehicle. I have a burning inside of me; it is growing, and I cannot turn it off. The burning goes from burn to sharp pain back to burn growing from my stomach, spreading and covering now my entire chest. I think to go to the hospital emergency to beg them to sedate me, anything to stop me from going to score. But I do not do this. In the car, driving on autopilot. I am not even thinking of where to drive; it is instead some strange entity, this burning that is now in control. My car pulls up to an all-too-familiar apartment building. My body glides somehow gracefully in distress. Buzzer pressed in the elevator before it has been five minutes, all anxiety and pain is gone as I begin jonesing for my second hit.

Today, I see my sobriety does have some semblance to the twelve steps—notably the higher power. But I never put these steps in my life consciously. I feel I have really been saved with no doing of my own; it was God who intervened.

Life evolved from an abyss of Godhood.
I was not in God, but I was in the hood.
With broken spirit I stood,
a fool fallen for the devil's intention.
Rescued only by desire,
I fulfilled prophecies of destruction.

I have just woken from two and a half solid days of sleeping. Who knows how long I had been without sleep till I finally was no longer able to make it back out my front door. I shower, dress, eat the remaining food in the cupboard, and head to my mother's house to hit her up for some groceries.

On my way driving to my mother's house, which is on the other side of town, I notice a helicopter in the sky traveling along the same route as the road I am driving. Later, I am with my mother driving and I notice the helicopter again. We visit my aunt. Leaving my aunt's house en route to the grocery store, "Look, isn't that the same helicopter?" my mother asks me. Oh shit, I am thinking, am I tripping or what? It seems this same helicopter has been directly above me all day anytime I have been in a vehicle. My mom and I enter a Price Chopper supermarket, and I pass off the helicopter to cocaine psychosis.

Shopping in the store, I am in an aisle looking at something on the shelf. I look to my left, and down the aisle, I see some guy staring at me. He notices me looking at him and picks something off the grocery shelf aimlessly. I walk away. In the next aisle, I see the same guy now with another man; they both catch me staring at them staring at me, and they quickly turn their attention back to the groceries. Next aisle, same guys, next aisle, same guys—what the fuck is going on?

I am with my mother, walking out of the store with grocery bags in both my hands, and I see some guy familiar around fifteen feet from me on a payphone. He sees me coming out the store and hangs up the phone and starts walking rapidly toward me. As soon as the guy is like seven feet away, two minivans pull out jumping the curb and men rush out the vehicles to surround me. "Drop the groceries. Hamilton PD. You are under arrest."

My mother is crying. "What are you doing? Why are you taking my son?"

"Your son is a drug dealer ma'am," the fat piece of shit undercover answers my crying mother. They cuff me, throw me in a minivan, and we drive away, leaving my mom at the curb outside the grocery store with groceries spilt everywhere at her feet. This is Hamilton's finest, and so much for innocent till proven guilty.

Driven into the underground garage of the Barton Street Jail and put in front of a cop at a desk where the top was level with my chin, I was searched and put in my cell. I am stretching out, trying to get comfortable on my metal bed, and *boom* I hear my buddy Sid being shuffled into the cell next to me. A moment later, "Aart" is put in a cell next to Sid. Apparently, four arrests were made—all simultaneous and in different parts of the region. Yes, they got the SW gang, all thanks to an undercover cop named Frenchie, the long-haired stoner with a limp. Unknown to us, we had been selling crack to this undercover for some months now. I remember the first time I met Frenchie; he looked at the crack with horror. You can't say he was chipping his own piece of the evidence as all the documented pieces of dope in court somehow diminished to half their size.

Nevertheless, Christmas and New Year's in jail that year was enlightening and at least sobering, to say the least. At that time, the jail was packed double capacity. I began my time sleeping on the concrete floor of a cell; each cell had two beds but at least three inmates.

One of the most interesting things I learnt about myself in jail was that I snored, as informed by my cell mates. No one wanted to share a cell with me. Within weeks, the bank robber and Chinaman I had as cell mates were now four in a cell elsewhere. The other inmates called me Devito, but all the guards called me the Penguin. Only the Penguin, in all the jail double capacity of four hundred plus prisoners, had a cell of his own. The guards didn't know who I was; they didn't know my privilege was just a result of my snoring. Some weeks later, the Chinaman would take his frustration out on me for losing his spot in a bed by attacking me in the jail kitchen. It was quite the incident. We are on the line making the food trays, and he, beside me, disappears. I'm wondering where the hell he went, now filling two compartments of the food trays instead of one. *Smack*! I am hit from behind with two broomsticks. The whole kitchen goes silent as the echo of the *smack* traveled from one end of the kitchen to another. I turn to see the Chinaman doing some karate stance, hissing at me like a little man possessed by a cat; my whole body is shaking. I want to just grab him and crush him to the ground. Before any thing else is possible, guards from everywhere appear. Seizing him, they carry him away. Chinaman is screaming. "Fuck you, Devito. You think you get out of jail, I make it so you don't get out." I see and understand it was a trick. A trick to try to get me to hit him so I would have to do more time. Wasn't going to happen. The warden comes down, and he and a guard take me in the stockroom, and they take pictures of the fresh welts on my back. I go back up to my range and shower; the other inmates are staring at me in amazement as they see I am not affected whatsoever by my welt marks. They are impressed. And this now is the beginning of a new problem; now they want to see Devito fight. And the next morning they are fresh on me telling me, "You see that guy, Neufie? Go fight him."

I am a big guy at this time in my life. I am one of those rare cases that actually puts weight on with crack. Yes, it is possible. I am about 230 lbs, and in jail, I have got up to three hundred push-ups every morning. But I am not the violent kind, the type of guy who would get hit ten times before I ever would think of punching back. But now the pressure is on. And if I don't fight this guy, I am in for big-time beats. I figure the best plan is to piss off Neufie to the point of him hitting me first; this might make it easier for me to get a reason to fight him. If only the guy would take my bait and hit me a few times. Problem is, he just seems to adore me, and when I get really rude with him, it just seems like he is going to cry but doesn't get angry. I drop all the cards and drop the biggest insult you can say in jail. I call him a "fucking goof." He looks at me expressionlessly and just walks away. "Yo, goof, I am talking to you!" He has just waved at me good-bye and is now on the other side of the range.

The range is in an uproar. This is not allowed to happen. No one is allowed to let anyone call them *goof* without hitting back. Some of the inmates have grabbed Neufie and dragged him up to me; they have his arms and are trying to get him to punch me, forcing his arms at me. At the same time, one or two guys are smacking him in the face like a bitch. "PENGUIN!" a guard shouts from the door of the range, "you're getting out, come on." Now that's what I call being saved by the bell.

There is one thing I did not mention about my time in jail, and that was the weekend chapel service we could attend. The first service I attended, we sang "Glory, Glory, Alleluia" and I broke down crying like a baby. It was these moments in jail at these services that I first felt a taste of the power of my religion—the saving power of the Holy Spirit. We would sing a hymn, something that went like this: "complete, complete, we are complete in him, we are complete in him, he is building an army and we are complete in him." I really forget how it went exactly, but when we would sing it, we would stomp our feet and sing at the top of our lungs, and just for a moment, none of us prisoners were in jail. Just for a moment, we were more free than the birds flying in the sky because, just for a moment, we could understand through feeling that what was most important was still intact inside of us. No guard and no jail could ever succeed in locking us away from the Lord. And it was the Lord in the end, and it was him in the beginning. As long as we had this, we could very well die in there and experience our creator as he meant it. Christmas in jail was the best ever, and New Year's was not the worst either.

Released from jail, I have my belongings back and exit on foot through the side gate. I have a lighter, a coat, and forty-something bucks. Another guy getting released at the same time as me gives me a smoke; I let him use my light. My God, that's the stalest smoke I ever enjoyed; what a head rush. I am walking down the street, thinking suddenly to walk to the nearest crack house to buy a forty piece, but I decide against it. I stop, use the payphone, call my mom, and decide to take a cab the fuck out of Hamilton. The next day, I already get a job as a line cook at some shit corporate restaurant, and the next week, with my first paycheck, I get high as a motherfuck on crack. It's not long till I am working the grill on a Saturday night rush, having not slept in three or four days. Man, I must have fucking ruined some poor bastard's Saturday night with the steaks and salmon I was putting out. Before my shift is over, I have made the salad girl cry and strangled the pivot cook with my apron strings. I throw my tongs against the wall; they bounce off the wall and hit the kitchen manager in the head. The next morning, I call in to work to quit and ask if they need notice. The manager politely sighs and tells me it's quite all right. "Just don't ever come back."

Cattle know who owns them, and donkeys know where their
master feeds them.
But that is more than my people know . . .
—ISAIAH 1:3

I am a driver. All I do is drive. Everyone is my friend because everyone
always needs a ride. In one day, I can make up to ten grams of crack
and around two hundred bucks cash. Yet at some point each day or
night, I am always broke—without gas and hungry. Always struggling to
stay awake, my dog and I living out of our car, now a red Volkswagen Jetta.
We are out of gas on the east side of Hamilton, and I have been awake
almost six days. I leave Shadow, my dog, locked in the backseat and begin
walking to the closest open gas station, jerry can in hand. All I remember
next is waking, bent over, next to a gas pump, nozzle in hand in the jerry
can. I had fallen asleep pumping gas. I look up at the gas attendant in the
kiosk staring at me in amazement. I slip back into sleep. I wake again. I pull
the gas nozzle to pump. I fall back to sleep then wake then sleep then wake.
Each time, the clanking noise of me releasing the pump trigger wakes me
back up. A good forty-five minutes pass, and I have pumped a good four
liters of gas into the jerry can. I place the gas nozzle back in its holder and
slowly walk toward the kiosk window. Now to deal with the attendant,
since I have no money to pay.

"Sir, I have to go back to my vehicle to get my wallet," I lie. "May I leave
you my license till I return?"

He motions to me to look at a drawer he opens; it is filled with hundreds
of driver's licenses. "No way, pal," he responds.

I plead, but he won't listen. Then I start ranting. "That's fuckin' fine, but this is my jerry can, so just tell me where you want me to dump this gas out."

"No problem, we have a bin for that." Oh shit, so much for that plan. I end up leaving my watch for the gas—I guess he likes the watch—and I begin my walk back to my car where my doggie is also waiting.

I am walking down Cannon Street in Hamilton, jerry can in hand; it is about four in the morning, and there is no one driving on the road except the occasional police cruiser. I walk and every minute or so begin to nod off. Falling asleep completely is very hard to do while walking but is possible if one is tired enough. I usually wake just as I am dozing and begin to fall and catch myself as I stagger. Losing my balance usually wakes me up; one time I actually hit the ground hard and woke abruptly, quickly securing my gas from spilling. The cruisers on the street always seem to be the same one and man I just want to get back to my doggie and car. At last at my vehicle, I cheer Shadow; he is excited and happy to see me. He is used to my insanity; it keeps me from going completely insane. He is a dog, a German shepherd, and is more intelligent than any crackhead in the city, and that includes me. Many times when I am driving, he ducks below the seat when a cop is near—as if to signal me—and keeps six better than anyone or anything I know. He is the only one out of the two of us who ever has food, and often he shares it with me. I remember one day realizing I had not eaten in three days, picking some chicken bones out of a garbage can near KFC for myself to eat. All they did was make me more hungry. I was then feeding Shadow, and his food looked so good while I watched him eat. I reached down and grabbed two fingers of it, tasted it, and it was awesome. Shadow looked at me strangely then sat back and motioned the dish toward me. He saw I was starving, and from that day, he always saved food in his dish for me. Seven years later, Shadow would be rewarded, as he only eats steak and the most expensive cheese with his food. As I am writing this book—this actual page—we just finished splitting three steaks between us. I owe more to a dog than any person; most of all, though, I thank God for putting this canine in my life, without whom I would have been dead ten times already.

We are in the car and driving. I am singing as loud as possible; this is how I stay awake. Next thing I know it is morning; the car is running, Shadow is licking my face. We are at a stop sign. One of my buddies, "Cube," is at my car window. "Black Rob, wake up, man. How long have you been sleeping here at this stop sign?" Wow, it's like seven in the morning. Just at that moment, the car dies. Out of gas again.

I wake up, and I am sleeping on the floor of Cube's apartment next to my dog. He is awake, watching me. All around us are our empty McDonald burger wrappers, at least ten or fifteen, and a bunch of hamburger buns. Shadow only eats the patties. Cube comes in the front door. He hands me the keys to my car and says for me to go meet a friend we both know—this guy who needs a ride to Toronto, about a one-hour drive. Cube hands me like a forty piece of crack to wake me up to get moving. I do it in three blasts and am off racing out the door with my dog to pick up the dealer and drive.

I have this guy in the front seat with me; let's just call him "C." The deal is, I drive him to Toronto; in exchange, he puts twenty bucks of gas in the tank and gives me twenty dollars cash and about a gram of crack. This is good to me, and Shadow is happy to be back home in the backseat of our car. I drop C off in the north end of Toronto before getting on the highway back to Hamilton. I pull down an empty road, park the car, leave Shadow for a bit, and sit in some bush, smoking my crack. I don't have a pipe though, and the pop can kind of sucks. I stop, all tripped out and not knowing what is normal for these parts I am in. Back in the car on the highway, we are flying down, speeding, and I begin nodding again. I guess I did not sleep enough. Just like that, and all of a sudden it's raining and thundering like nuts. We are around three minutes away from Hamilton, and I pull over on the side of the highway. The rain stops. I stand out the car, put all the remaining crack I have on my shitty pop can, and hit that bitch. *Buzzzzzzzzzzzzzzzzzzzzzzzzz.* Holy! I stamp on the can flat and toss it in the bush. I am back in the car, but before I even start it, I am sleeping again.

Its probably been like an hour and there is a knocking at my car window. Shadow barks and growls; it's the OPP. "Officer, I am out of gas and waiting for a tow truck," I lie to the police officer. He goes on his way. I fall back to sleep. About an hour or two later, there again is another cop at my window. I give him the same story and he leaves. I get out of my car, open my gas cap door, and figure this should be like a "do not disturb" sign for the cops. I am back in my vehicle, me and the dog snug in our filth. A few hours later, I walk Shadow along the highway to shit; he eats his food out of the trunk. I find a week-old piece of pizza in the trunk as well and chew it, pulling the dog hair off it only once they are in my mouth. Shadow and I rest and eat like crackhead kings and head back into the city.

Lies

This is like the fourth or fifth time I am in this rehab: Nonsensenon in Quebec. The first time I was here I got so fuckin' sick, and the fuckin' French doctor just kept on saying "virus, virus, virus." We could only get to the doctor once a week, and they minivan us to this doctor an hour-and-a-half drive away. I was sick arguing with their support lady. I remember that day: everyone on the doctor run got Buckley's. But not only did I not, but neither did I get my medicine that had taken three weeks and three doctor visits to get prescribed. I come down into the cafeteria for lunch and I snap, kicking the garbage can from one end of the cafeteria to the other; the whole place—full of clients and staff—goes silent. Brad Janes yells at me, "Go upstairs, your medicine is here."

"About fucking time!" I scream. "I have only been sick three weeks, I still want fucking out of this place."

I go back upstairs; the lady wants to argue more with me. We call her No-Anne. I mean it's one big power trip at this rehab. They want us to be like five year olds and they know best, but what they think they know is that if we get sick we are not sick because of illness or infection or disease per se. They believe all illness is a result of being effected by another person or our past "suppression."

"I will give you your medicine, but first I want you to sit down and speak with me and see that I am not wrong, but I am right," the lady says to me when I appear back at her office door. I am livid. The other lady working the support office merely shrugs her head and looks down on the floor. She sees I am terribly ill. She sees what is going on, but I guess she sees her job too.

"Just give me my fucking antibiotics. I am not going to argue with you, nor listen to you. It's not about if you are right or wrong, all I want is my antibiotics! I don't have to listen to you to get them," I say.

The next two days, sick as hell, I am trying to leave, but they will not give me my ID. Finally fed up, I sit at the computer and start sending out emails to any newspaper or television news agency I can find on the net, asking them to get a hold of me at the name of the rehab. Just as I am doing this, Brad Janes sees me and asks what I am doing. I tell him simply, "If I am not out of here by 2 p.m. today, this whole place is going to be crawling with television cameras and reporters."

Not twenty minutes go by and I am in a minivan with my possessions en route to the Trois-Rivieres bus station.

So I do return to this rehab after I relapse because the cross with Jesus on it buzzes my cell phone. I take it as a sign to return; after all, I never did finish their program. I had been clean for a couple months, which at that point was one of the best clean runs for me. I decide to return to give it a second try. I am told that the success rate for graduates who finish is like 70 percent; I later see it in my own eyes that this 70 percent is at best the failure rate.

I come back in a November, and it is January now the next year and I am just finishing the program. I think I am like one of the first program completions in 2009. It is suggested I do a certain exercise to get more comfortable with drugs if ever I do come back in contact with them; it is called "reach and withdrawal."

A few hours pass and I am in the executive boardroom of the rehab; the man who walks in was one of my course room instructors. He has a cardboard box in his hands like about the size big enough to fill his arms. He sits the box on the boardroom table where I am sitting, and he begins pulling the contents of this box out onto the table. First, a forty of beer, then it looks like a bottle of hard liquor. Then it starts, baggie after plastic baggie of every and any drug imaginable. I was a fucking crackhead, and yes, there must be like at lest five different baggies of just crack alone. I mean, some of this crack must be old; I can tell by how it looks, losing its moisture content: white crack, beige crack, big boulder crack, powder crack, cocaine, and what all these fucking pills are in these other bags I have no fucking idea. Plus ginseng glass pipes and stems all caked in resin. But I mean—man! Today still, when I crave sometimes, I still think of that fucking cardboard box!

He asks me if I am well-fed or tired or if there is any reason why not to start, then we begin. Can you say Star Trek Enterprise? I mean, are these people really from fucking Pluto or what? I mean they must have no sense of reality about drug addiction! Here I am about to go home in a day or two, not yet three months clean, and they want me to handle crack and pipes! He starts the exercise by saying to me, "Reach for that crack!"

I reach out for a baggie of crack and handle it in my hands. I feel its hardness; I imagine melting it. He interrupts my thought: "Withdrawal from that crack!" I put it back down on the table. He goes on, "Reach for that pipe!" Wow, I reach out and pick up a glass pipe; my mind is slobbering over that dry cake full of beautiful resin. "Withdrawal from that pipe!" I mean, this goes on and on for like about thirty minutes. After a while, my eying of the drug as a drug stops. I turn to him and say something like "I am here and these drugs and pipes are in my space, but they are not really in my space. I mean I can reach for this pipe, but I can also crush it!"

He says, "Good, end of session." They certify me a graduate; I feel great. Five days later, I relapse: my shortest clean run ever after a rehab. Why would I ever go back to that rehab a third time? The honest answer: I have no fucking idea, but I do. Again and again and even again. Each time I go back after relapse, they say it was something I did wrong in my previous program. You see, when you succeed according to them, it is because of their program. And of course, when you fail, it is all your fault. These godless sons of bitches! Don't they know that it's me, the addict, who has everything to lose here? Meaning my life—they are playing with people's lives, hopes, and dreams. They say if I complete the program I am no longer an addict, meaning I will no longer crave. So today I am clean over a year, and I still have thoughts. For me, it is knowing my weakness that delivers me from it. They did not teach me this; what they taught me I put on a shelf and labeled it "the past." Do not get me wrong. Rehabs are not a bad place, and even this rehab is, per se, not a bad place. Every addict needs a starting point, just a place to clean up.

When I left this place the second time, I am back home in Ontario, driving with my dog Shadow. It is around 11 p.m. on a Sunday evening; the video game I was playing was boring me. I thought, I'll just go out and buy a fifty piece and that's it. I have no fear of the drug. Big mistake. My first toke at an old buddy's place with his girlfriend, and for one moment, the whole world seems perfect. But then it was not perfect, and each next toke is just a fleeting hope in the wrong. A day, a night, another day, another night, a week and then another week—its an endless and relentless pursuit of what it is I don't know. But all this dope is just a pipe dream, and my body begins withering as my dog sighs at me: "failure."

When I return a third time to this rehab in Trois-Rivieres, they call me upstairs to an executive office to talk. I have been commenting to them that it was their fault I relapsed. Also, the press are still calling from what went on a year ago. The lady I am talking to suggests that I am merely blaming others for my failure. She says, "I would suggest you have no integrity."

"Look, lady," I stare her down and say, "when I put that pipe in my mouth, I have zero integrity, and I am the first to know it."

Now another couple years later, I did complete that program again and then again, and I am clean. And truly I would not be clean today if I had not gone back again and again. But don't assume, Mr. and Mrs. Rehab, that you have all the answers and that your fancy formulas are magic. Almost each day, I have a sense of my old addiction in some way. It is life that teaches me and the support of God. No cookie-cutter rehab program can take the credit; all they can truly take is their fee.

Buick on Fire

I am driving this old blue 1980 Buick. I have been clean for a few days, and just bought the car of "Fats" for three hundred bucks. I am hoping it lasts me two weeks. I have been driving for like twenty minutes now; I am in a bad part of town, and the engine is overheating big time. I can feel the heat of the engine through the vents, and I am blasting the heat so to help push out the hot air. Just as I am turning left through a busy intersection, all I hear is a *BAMMM*!

Its like the car almost exploded, and now streams of smoke are coming out from everywhere near the engine. The engine is running, and it's revving harder and harder. The dashboard is like an oven, and the vehicle is now screaming loudly. I jump from the car and pull Shadow out from the backseat. People in cars on all ends of the intersection are stopped and blocked by me; they are staring in disbelief as to what they are seeing. In movies, you see people in such scenarios scream and yell at such a delay, but probably in fear of the state I appear in, all these people just stare with their jaws dropped. I just start sprinting from the car with my dog. I turn back and see that the vehicle is now in flames, burning away in the middle of the intersection. Fuck it, I figure, and turn back toward the opposite direction and continue running. I know Dan has a crack spot just five blocks from here, and I still have a wad of cash in my pocket.

So I get to Dan's. Shadow runs up the stairs to Dan's bedroom, and Dan takes his leash. "Black Rob, leave Shadow with me for a bit." I buy about three hundred bucks worth of crack and venture through the rest of the house. It is like a crack cocktail party.

Crackhead ho bitches everywhere, with poor young lads who have to run out for deliveries for tokes. There is one chicky—let's just call her "Chicky." She goes out to do a delivery almost every hour. When she does, she is dressed as a jogger. From afar, you would never smell her stench. I am on the couch, and the house phone rings. It is Fats; he is on the phone and is furious. I guess the Buick was still registered to him and was found burning in the middle of an intersection. Oh well, my party continues. Hours and hours go by; I finish my crack and hang with the dog and Dan. I fall asleep with Shadow waiting for Dan to re-up.

I wake with Shadow on Dan's bed. For a moment, I do not know where I am; everything is the same but the whole house is completely different in its sound. There is no sound; there is no one. I do not think there is anybody else in the house. Then suddenly I hear "mhmhmhhaaaaaaaaaaaa!" A distant muffled scream. I am not sure if it is from this house or the next one. I get up with Shadow and slowly descend the stairs to the first floor. The person I hear—it sounds like it is coming from the basement. I leave Shadow in the living room for a moment and peek into the basement.

"Heelllllllllp meeeeeeeeeee!" I hear the voice more clearly; it is that of a man. I go halfway down the stairs now and peer around and see, tied to a support beam of the house, some poor mother fucker in his underwear. He is tied up real good and looks like he has already received a beating. I don't recognize him, and there is no way I am untying him. I mean, this is Dan's house and nothing goes on in Dan's house without him knowing. So if this poor motherfucker is tied up and beaten—so be it. I run back into the kitchen, use the phone to call Fats. "Ya, I left the Buick in the intersection, it fucking exploded. No, I have no money left. Come pick me and Shadow up."

Fats knows better than to come within one hundred yards of one of Dan's spots—they are much too hot for him—so I run with Shadow five or six blocks toward downtown to get picked up. Back to the scrap yard to find my burnt Buick. As I run out of the front of Dan's house, I am taken aback by the sight of schoolchildren all walking home happily from school. In the distance of my mind is some poor motherfucker beaten and tied to a pole, screaming, as kids get home for the after-school snacks with Mommy. Each house door is the same, but beyond inside each one is such a different world.

Police arrest dealers and put them in jail, once so often doing sweeps of the city. The result usually is they just make room for a younger generation of dealers usually from the next bigger city—more violent, more cruel. Originally in Hamilton, say fifteen years ago, there was a group of older dealers who, besides dealing crack, had set rules for conduct. They have long been all removed. As years went, on the dealer has devolved into a younger bunch, mostly from Toronto, who cares not. I have seen a dealer break a woman's finger over a five-dollar debt. The only comical thing with this bunch is how paranoid they are of being robbed. Hence, the reason for knives and guns.

Crack cliques or gangs (whatever you want to call them), bands of robbers, usually a group of crackheads who have survived together on the streets for some years—they regard themselves as a family. It is a street family, but do not let the use of the word *family* fool you; it is not like you may know the word. These people will befriend you just to knife you in the back. If they are desperate enough in a moment, they will rob someone of their last few dollars then throw them up and out of the crack spot for making noise. They will rat you out to die, worse than to the police, and instead set you up to be robbed—or worse, when it's time, beat you just to set an example. It is amongst these people that I earned the name of "Black Rob," for after years and years of smoking crack, an essence of my character was revealed. Then I was called Robin the Hood, but that I could persist with the best of them and yes even rob a fellow myself, but I preferred to take rather than steal.

I remember my first days of smoking crack in the inner city of Hamilton, locked up in some third-floor apartment on Barton Street: two rooms and a kitchen, two black dealers from Toronto, and they know I have bucks. I have been smoking up in their clutches for something like three days now. I am by myself in this world.

All are sleeping, and I am in a room with a bed, three people asleep on it plus two on the floor. It is completely dark. I can hear a young blond girl on the bed; she is crying. I approach her; she wipes her tears. She cannot be more than sixteen years old; they call her "Sunshine." She tells me how she had been paid fifty dollars for giving one of the dealers a blowjob, then after while she was sleeping, he came and took the fifty bucks back. She was awake but let him take it, pretending she was sleeping; she was terrified. Just as she is telling me this, there is a banging at the door. Someone opens the door; it is the police. Sunshine tells me to pretend I am sleeping. About three or four cops come in the room with flashlights. They move their lights over our faces and over our pipes and paraphernalia. They walk out of the apartment just as they came in; they don't care. This is all our own problem of our own making and resolving; the police are not there to help, just enforce political agenda. I remember when some international bike race came to the city; the police cracked down and arrested every working girl just for that weekend. As soon as the race was over, they were all back on the streets. A fuckin' joke.

Anyway, so I have to leave this apartment and go home. It's been four days now, and my plan is to return in the morning with more money. Everyone in the apartment knows this.

Come morning, I am walking up the back entrance of the building, and "Cath" sees me and hollers at me to come in her apartment first. My dealer friend was supposedly already in her place waiting for me. Cath was an older—about in her late forties—mulatto lady with an afro who was known for her anger. I run into her place through the backdoor, entering the kitchen. I close the door and turn to see seven crackheads approaching me. "Quick, grab him." I hear Cath scream.

I try to turn back toward the door, but I am pinned by all their bodies, and the door opens inward, so all of our weight is preventing me from getting out. I suddenly roar and push, and they are all flying across the room like bowling pins down on the ground. Just as this happens—"Hold him, get the knife, stab him"—Cath screams.

The door is awkward, and I can't get it open. I turn back to see Cath lunging at me with a butcher knife, one person who at that point I don't even know. "Terr," he jumps in front and trips her, throwing her to the ground. He stands in front of me to stop the next person approaching with a knife. I am out the door, sprinting as fast as I can down Barton Street. I run around ten blocks without even looking back; when I do, I see this guy who just saved my life just a half a block behind.

I knew Terr for years after; he is eventually put in a wheelchair by a dirty needle fix delivered into his vein by another junkie. Years later, you can tell right away if it's a crack house when you see Terr's wheelchair parked just outside the front door. They usually just leave the chair outside and carry him in and leave him at the kitchen table.

"Hey, Rob, I know you, you are Sel's friend. I'll take you someplace safe." I follow him, and he takes me to another third-floor apartment, this one on a corner near Wentworth. This apartment seems much calmer, but after moments of Terr and I arriving, there seems to be more and more people in the place. I am sitting in a room in a circle with some others, all who I don't know. I have a terrible feeling inside. I am still stuck in the moment when I was attacked not more than hour ago. I think the same thing is going happen again. I quietly ask a girl beside me if I may borrow her cell phone; she obliges. I call Sel's number.

I quietly speak into the phone. "Sel, I think I am about to be robbed." He asks where I am. I ask the girl if she could speak to my friend; she does.

Less than ten minutes have passed; we are all seated still in a circle now on the floor of the living room. I do a toke, and just as I was exhaling, the front door of the place smashes inward. Sel files through the door into the apartment with four others, each brandishing baseball bats; they just begin randomly selecting people and beating them with the bats. Gato, one of Sel's friends, motions me out of the apartment. I quickly walk out. All I can hear is the sound of bats hitting bones and the wailing of whoever was in the place.

I am quickly walked down the street a few blocks to another apartment. There, I sit with Sel and his buddies, and I stay for some five or six days with them. Sel does not smoke from a pipe but instead crumbles his crack in tobacco and smokes it like a joint: we call these zukes. "You see this man?" Sel says to someone, talking of me. "For five days, he has been staring into the sun, and still his face is not burnt." Whatever he was saying, I took it as a compliment. Sel is kind enough to drive me home after my money is done. I have him drop me a few moments from my buddy's home. The only thing better than a dealer who delivers is one who will drive you home once you're broke and broken. Before he drives me home, he buys me some Chinese food. I cannot eat it. I cannot remember the last time I ate. I try one battered shrimp. I barely am able to swallow it, and it feels stuck in my esophagus. He motions for me to drink some of his pop. I have a sip; now it feels like this battered shrimp is expanding with the moisture in the middle of my esophagus. With each second, it feels bigger and bigger. I jump out of Sel's car and make my way to the side door of my buddy's house; I make it down to his basement. He looks at me in horror. In about a week, I probably dropped around twelve pounds—not only was I not eating but also barely drinking. I am so tired, I collapse on his basement rec room couch in exhaustion.

It's about five in the morning. I awake from my first hour of sleep in at least a week. I look up and see my buddy's mom staring down at me. "Have you seen Spinny or Awesome? You are not on top of them, are you?" She's talking about her cats, but I don't know this at the time. She is circling the couch I am on. "Here, Awesome. Here, Spinny." I am freaking out. "Look, Mrs.—, I don't know what's going on, but I am sleeping for the first time in a long time. But now that you are here, I may need you to drive me to the emergency 'cause I think I have a battered shrimp stuck in my esophagus." She motions like she hears something upstairs and leaves the room. Must think I am nuts. I fall back to sleep or better call it oblivion.

The scariest thing for me after not sleeping for days and days was sleeping itself. Anything not to sleep. It's like after being up a few days, the body forgets what it is or how to fall asleep. The body confuses falling to sleep with death itself. Sleep becomes the same as for a fish going out of water, and my spasms are quite similar. This is called the "flip flop."

Alive but on drugs, you sense some strange sensations. Your mind is so working in overdrive. Sometimes, for only a moment, you can stare right into what you think is heaven and, some other moments, hell. While high, I have met Satan himself; also quite a few angels indeed. Some feelings you can never shake, and sad to say, it was those moments of perception of light and darkness that make what is dark and what is light so easily identifiably to me now. Worse, for reality, it was not always a place with drugs that was some of the darkest dark I have seen. Actually, some rehabs take the cake for being the darkest places.

Sleep Driving While Dreaming Chinese Food

I wake up in my car, Shadow in the backseat beside me. In the passenger seat, some girl is sleeping, and the car is moving around fifty kilometers an hour. We are going down the mountain brow road, a steep declining road that winds around the edge of the Hamilton Escarpment. Forget sleepwalking, this is sleep driving.

I wake the girl up; she says last she remembers I was awake and she nodded. I figure I have been driving at least twenty minutes but while asleep, this is all through daytime traffic. Other times similar, I remember a forty-minute drive and only being conscious for five or ten minutes of that time, the rest of the drive a coming to and falling out of consciousness, constantly waking finding myself past turns and so on, making a fifteen-minute drive last almost an hour. Literally, some drives that should of taken me thirty minutes have taken a full day, constantly falling asleep and passing turns, sometimes saved by running out of gas and drifting to a halt.

I am exhausted, and that is an understatement. I get to where I was driving, and Shadow and I with the girl go into Fats's spot. Once on his couch, I am out, sleeping in seconds. Fats is a tall but very fat, over four hundred pounds, Italian friend of mine. High blood pressure, asthma, a heart condition, sleep apnea: he sleeps with a mask on. When I would go visit him for dope when he was sleeping, entering his bedroom was like approaching Darth Vader commingled with Jaba the Hut, this big mountain of rolls of a person with heavy breathing in stereo sound. Often, he would spill his whole bag of dope on himself in the bed and just fall back to sleep, occasionally stirring to me picking up forty dollar-sized boulders out of his bedsheets as he slept.

Fats was a gambler. I remember being with him in the falls. In less than the time it took me to smoke a ball of crack in my motel room, he would already be back to my room, returned from the casino after having lost all his money plus his re-up money. I looked at him and told him maybe he should give up gambling and start smoking crack: it would be cheaper. The next morning, that deposit of the TV remote got us home.

I wake some hours later. I am sitting on Fats's couch, up right with a dish of Chinese food on my lap, half of it spilt on my chest. I eat the food off my chest and stomach with my hands and fall back to sleep. I stay on the couch for about two days; I don't remember much. Apparently, I am quite the spectacle houseguest and attraction. Fats's friends come over just to get a look at me. They bring me food and sit and watch me sit up, eat, and return to lying down all in my sleep. Occasionally, I wake and see mobsterlike dudes just sitting around the coffee table next to me, staring at me, jaw dropped. I am told they have full conversations with me while I am sleeping. I eat donuts and bowls of pasta in my sleep. I am told I even drank half of a coffee with them all while I never woke.

I wonder if Shadow sleep-eats as well. Did I have the Chinese food or just dream it? No. I look at my shirt: definitely was Chinese and definitely not a dream.

Time goes by at no cost to my soul.
I broil my ideas to last in this fridge longer,
but the door won't shut.
And the power bill, God won't pay.

I am returning to Dan's spot in Hamilton to smoke some tokes with his girls and maybe drive a bit. On my way up the backstairs of his apartment building, I see "Q," a pretty brunette crackhead. If there is such a thing, she is it. We walk through the door of Dan's apartment, and we see around five or six people, all standing and sitting silently. Dan is sitting on the edge of his bed directly across from some guy who I don't know; he is seated in a chair facing Dan hands concealed between his legs. The guy who I don't know looks at me and seems to recognize me; he gives me a second glance. Suddenly, Dan charges from his seated position and tackles buddy. At last, I figure out the seriousness of the situation as I see from in between the mystery person's legs a gun goes flying up in the air. Both mystery man and Dan's hands are on the gun, and as Mystery is struggling, Dan is forcing the butt of the gun, hitting Mystery in the head with it once, twice, three times. Now Mystery is against the closed door of the apartment. He does not have hold of the gun anymore, and Dan is repeatedly smacking the butt of the gun against the top of the guy's head. Everyone is running around in the apartment, screaming, except for me. I am just standing completely still in the midst of the chaos. Mystery is, somehow, still on his feet and has made it back across to the other side of the apartment and is out on the balcony. Someone locks the balcony door.

Dan is moving toward the balcony door with the gun, and someone yells, "Cops are coming!" Next thing I know, I am driving, and I have Dan and two others with the gun in the car along with my dog. They want to look for Mystery's friend who made off with all the crack. It's a hopeless pursuit, driving down city streets looking for some guy—who knows who he is? I haven't done a toke in a while, but who needs drugs when guns are flying in the air? The one who made it away still has a gun as well. I am relieved when Dan decides to give up looking. We go back to Dan's apartment. Mystery is no longer there, and the cops never came. For the next three days, the dog and I drive Dan around to all his crack spots, and we are on high alert. At any moment, we know either Mystery or his friend could be back trying to finish what they started. These guys are from the East End of town and have been apparently robbing everyone in other parts of the city, and they haven't met trouble till they tried to rob Dan. There are more of them than just the two, and we be living in the West Side. Now it seems I may have stepped into a little crack clique grudge thing.

Man see steel.

Man must taste steel.

—old saying

It has been around five days since the robbery, and I for some stupidest reason ever, decide after dropping Shadow at home, to visit a crack house on the East Side to get high some more. Everything is cool, and all are having blasts quite literally. I am on the second floor of the house, chilling with some fat Italian guy named Bubs. I think Bubs has my back; boy, am I wrong.

I am seated on a couch. It is the summer months, and all the windows are open, dirty white drapes blowing about. I hit my pipe and lie back, enjoying something like a buzz during which I see a figure climb through a window and emerge from the drapes. It is Mystery, and he is smiling from ear to ear, or should I say from bump to bump on his head. That's not what I am focusing on though: it is, instead, the knife in his hand as he approaches me with his big smile and knife.

Bubs yells, "Ah he's got a knife, I hate knives!" He runs out the room and stands at the doorway. He just keeps screaming like a fat man with no balls, jumping from one leg to another. Me, I am stunned and scared shitless. This is it, I think, I am done. It seems Mystery doesn't necessarily want to kill me, or at least, not yet. Instead, he informs me he is only taking me hostage for now. He walks me out of the house, knife to my throat, and down the street, knife brandished and all, no one calls the cops. No one cares; you gotta love Hamilton.

He instructs me where to drive. I think of running out the car, but I don't. We are now in some alley somewhere, and he tells me to stop the car. He pulls the keys and leaves me in the car. Some chick comes out of a doorway, and they are talking. They start hugging and kissing, then she gives him a full smack to the head, then a closed fist. He hits her back, and she hits him back. All of a sudden, I realize what is happening: she's getting him going on purpose. Getting him into a rage so he can do me in.

Holy shit! I am fucked. They are both nuts and more nuts, and they approach the door. I am trying to stuff my wallet in my underwear as they approach me. Next thing I know, I am being pulled out of my car through the open window. I fall out the car, get up to stand, and hear my wallet hit the ground. Next thing, Chicky is on top of the car and jumps off at me; leg extended, she flying kicks me in my side. Now if I would say this hurt I would not be telling the truth because I guess it was, in fact, so painful that my sense of pain did turn off at that moment. How would I know this? Well I have Mystery now pulling me back to my feet, and every time I am up on my feet, he hits me with one of his fists. Each time he hits me, I see bright cameralike flashes. These flashes are all I can sense—no pain. Each time I fall to the ground like my knees are not working, each time he pulls me up again and hits me more—more flashes. To the ground again, again up, again down.

Finally, he turns from me. I pick myself up and run; and man do I run. I have no idea how fast I am running but I am running as fast as I can. Minutes later—no glasses, no wallet, no vehicle—I am in a variety store. The clerk jumps to his feet when I walk in and is on the phone calling 911. I guess I must look pretty bad. I ask him for a drink, and he gives me a plastic bottle of water. A cruiser pulls in, and I explain to the cop I was carjacked and beaten. The cop asks me who it was; "mystery to me," I say. I get a free ride home by the cop. I don't remember still how I got in my place, but man was I happy to curl up with Shadow. I sleep with my dog on the couch for three days, waiting for my face to get back to being presentable before I go back out.

Black Tricky and Juliette.
He caught her on the street when she was young—
tied her up and fed her crack
while him and seven of his friends had their fun.

I am the guest of honor. I am in a crack apartment on Victoria Street in Hamilton. Me and my buddy Gato walked up to the place to smoke some with Juliette, a cute mulatto girl. Just as we are approaching the door, we see just ahead of us Black Toronto "Tricky" and his friend, some slim black guy as well from Toronto. They are about to barge in the apartment. As they go in, we can hear Juliette screaming. We rush in and see Tricky brandishing a bloody sword, Juliette running about the apartment, screaming. On the couch is Counch, a tough white skinhead from the mountain, and he is bent over, bleeding bad. On the floor, on his knees, is Counch's driver begging, crying, pleading to Tricky's friend for his life. Tricky turns and sees me.

"Black Rob, welcome. Tonight you are the guest of honor." He pulls a chair facing Counch who is nearly passed out on the couch now. Tricky hands me like four grams of crack and says, "This is on the house." I have no choice but to sit in this chair and smoke this crack taken from Counch. In front of Counch, as he slips back in and out of consciousness, Tricky says, "No one leaves till morning." So I begin pacing my tokes over the hours while listening to his driver who has been forced to lie on his stomach face down; all he does is whimper.

That night was some time ago, and I am remembering it as I am told by Dan that Tricky was killed just weeks prior when robbed by Mystery. Last

I heard, Mystery was in jail. I never ran into him again. Dan might have. I know Dan did and got both run over and shot in the foot. Dan got away; I am not sure if Mystery was involved in this. Thank God Dan did get away, 'cause it is Dan in the end who finally drives me to my last visit to rehab. That time, I remembered my soul and to who it really belonged to.

I do meet Counch again. I am at Duff's Corners just outside Ancaster, now part of Hamilton, waiting for some unknown crack dealer a friend had arranged to send to meet me. I am in the gas station parking lot sitting in my car. I have twenty bucks and a case of twenty-four beers. Some little jeep pulls up; the driver motions me. I jump out of my vehicle into the little jeep with the beer and twenty-dollar bill. Inside the jeep is a shriveled, wrinkled-up Counch who is now half the size I remember him to be. He is nodding; he begins to doze just as I am getting in the jeep, but then is woken by some sort of nauseous pain. He is needle sick.

His cell phone rings; he answers and begins listening. As he does, he starts to nod asleep again. I am sitting in his jeep with the case of beer on my lap. Counch is in the driver's seat, jeep running, he is sleeping while on the phone. He is so skinny now, pale—a sick white with boils on his face and arms. He wakes suddenly in some sort of awesome pain then begins to nod again until the pain wakes him back. He keeps keeling forward, seemingly with pain in the stomach. He is no person, just a set of eyes with hurt.

Duff's Corners is a highway cross section with a twenty-four hour gas station and truck stop restaurant. Nearby suburbia encroaches with its smooth pavement and hollow streetlights; Walmart looms in the distance.

Conch cannot drive anymore; he is too sick. I put him in my truck and drive him to finish his deliveries, then bring him back to his jeep. He calls someone to come and meet him back at his jeep to drive him who knows where.

Conch and I were always happy to see each other after that night. Neither him nor me ever mentioned to anyone the bloody stabbing incident the first time we met. I guess both of us knowing that and both of us seeing each other just made us realize how lucky we were to be still alive. A reminding grace, actually—happy to still be living.

Crack-Mas with Dealer-Clause

It is a special day today. It is a special night tonight. It is Christmas, but just like any other day in that time, I am trapped in addiction. Now on Victoria Street in Hamilton, a basement apartment of some terrifically fat slob who somehow has the same name as me.

If I am trapped in addiction, let's say this apartment is trapped in the year 1982 or some year like that. Television, music, microwave—nothing has changed in this place in a good twenty years at least. There is food though, and Shadow is comfortably set up on the back porch entrance. The whole bunch of us are eager as Sel comes in with Christmas gifts: a forty piece for each of us all. Sel is not gone for ten minutes, and I am finished with my piece and jonesing.

I had left him my car, and Shadow and I are stuck in this place for who knows how long; there is around four or five of us here. This fat bastard is definitely high on something other than crack, and he is dancing around his apartment in circles, no shirt on, to some eighties rock music, his ass hanging out. His friend and him look like they are doing a choo-choo train around the living room. I pass the hours doing the occasional delivery for a few tokes, but my mood is slipping. At last I snap, freaking out on everyone, screaming.

Not five minutes during Sel's return, Shadow and I take off down a back-alley. I have the keys to my car, but I leave it parked and am on foot with my dog. It is about eleven on Christmas Eve. I am lost. I find myself at the steps of some church. I pause and sit on the steps, Shadow beside me. I try the door to the Church; it is locked. I sit back on the steps, looking up at the church then surveying the back alleyway that led me here. Christmas rings in silently void of all except my dog, then I am crying. I am on the steps alone but with my dog. I am in tears, freezing, sitting on cement. I am locked out of Christmas, locked out of Jesus, locked out of myself. A few hours pass, and I return to the fat bastard's apartment. I look around at everyone festively toking away. Sel is happy to see me and Shadow back, but something inside me tells me to leave. I am exhausted, broken inside. I drive a few minutes to another apartment, this one on Duke Street. This one is quiet, just the schizophrenic Chinese guy whose apartment it is. My head is pounding; all of a sudden I need to lie down.

I wake on buddy's couch. Shadow lying on the floor beside me, it is the middle of early morning. Buddy is wrapping my head with cold wet towels and ice. I am sweating profusely and cannot stop shaking. Everything in me is rattling, and all my body is pain. I don't know what is happening, what has come over me. All turns back to darkness that resembles sleep.

I wake up; it is a perfectly sunny morning, and I now feel fine. "Shadow and I thought we were going to lose you last night," the Chink says. All I remember is being on the couch, head in absolute pain, not being able to move, just shaking. And me, I just kept thinking about my mom and how she may be spending her Christmas. I look again outside to the sunny morning, bright snow shining back at a blue sky, and it is Christmas Day morning. I clean up the best I can in Chink's washroom and then drive back to where my mother is living. She feeds me and Shadow; we sleep for days.

I later find out from Chink that in the wee hours of Christmas morning while he was taking care of me on his couch that a fight had broken out at Fat Bastard's apartment. Just after I left, apparently Sel also left, then chaos ensued. Another dealer who arrived was beaten to within inches of his life for his crack. The dealer crawled home to his girlfriend. The girlfriend, enraged, paid a visit right back to the fat bastard's apartment brandishing a sword and stabbed up two people in the apartment, puncturing the lungs of one of them. Maybe it was God who guided me away that night, who froze me in pain and fever, really keeping me safe. Maybe it was my tears on the steps of that church that saved me. I wonder if that fat bastard ever put his shirt on before or after he had to clean up the blood.

Over the years, Christmases were spent in parks, church parking lots, jail, and of course, rehab. I rejoice on Christmas now. Truly, I believe God came for us imperfect bastards. And because why? Not because we deserved it, but because God loves us and truly wants each and every one of us to be saved.

If I did not love
My sin would not hurt
So only love in the end
Will stop me from sin
Love must be put into the moment now
And it must be like my lungs and heart
Love must be that thing that drives and stirs and guides.
Only love—nothing else.
Only then, perfect action,
Fearless peace.

I am in crack slums apartment building of Emerald Street near Main in Hamilton. I have been up for a good seven days with no sleep. I am in a ground-floor apartment where some retarded old man lives with his delinquent son. The old man is out; the son is half out of it in sleep. I am tisic and just lost a package of crack. All right, I have to find this. I tell everyone that no one can leave till I find the package I dropped. Everybody plays dumb. When you drop crack and no one helps you look for it, it only means one thing: everybody knows you dropped it, and everyone already smoked it or knows it has been found and smoked. You are a fool if you keep looking for it.

Someone is on the phone. I notice that, and after about ten minutes, I hear a vehicle pull up to the back. I know what is going on; I make for the backdoor to get out. As I am out the door and trying to make it to my car around the front of the building, I see around four or five guys jumping out of a vehicle. They are approaching me. I stop and turn toward them. Big mistake. Before anything could be said, I am sucker punched, and my glasses go flying off. I am saying, "Just let me find my glasses, then we can fight." All of them just keep hitting me time after time. After the first or second, or maybe it was the third or fourth shot to my head, I kind of phase out. I am still conscious, but I can't remember anything really. Next thing I know, I am on the ground, and I have my arms around my head. They are all around me, trying to kick me in the head. There feet are bouncing off my arms, then *BOOM* a foot must have hit me good in the head because all I know is coming to a few hours later at the side of the slum building. Some crackhead bitch was poking at me, trying to wake me up and see if I can go get her dope.

I come to and jump up crazy-mad like a madman. I am screaming. I jump in the car and begin driving through the city really fast, and that's an understatement. I know where I am going; I am going to get more crack. It's like I am possessed, screaming at no one as I am driving. I must be doing around 120 km in a 50 zone. I run a red light and get T-boned, lose control of the vehicle, jump the medium, and blow both left tires. I am still driving, thinking I can still get to the crack, but with only two right wheels, it's not going to happen. I abandon the vehicle and think maybe I can run the rest of the way. I turn and see I now have people chasing me on foot. Cops are coming. I fall on my butt to the ground.

I talk with the cop and tell him I was jumped downtown and was trying to make it back to a friend's house in a panic. He puts me in a tow truck and tells me to go with the tow truck driver to central station and fill out an accident report. I am in central station filling out a form at a desk in the traffic office. Next thing I know, everything goes dark.

I wake looking up at least six or seven police officers staring down at me; they are looking at me in disbelief. I can't move, or at least, I am too tired to try; everything is aching—most of all, my head. Next thing I know, they are putting me on a stretcher. Those were the friendliest cops I ever do remember. From the station, I am put in an ambulance. Next time I wake, I am in a hospital bed.

I am told I suffered a concussion and am told I am not to eat. No one is allowed to visit except family, and my friend Fats comes to see me, saying he is my cousin. I am sleeping when he visits; I wake and found a note he left and a twenty-dollar bill. I know the other guy in the room with me; he is a crackhead too. His arm is badly broken. He was trying to break into his mother's house. He had broken a window, and while reaching his arm in to turn the knob, his mother's boyfriend took a baseball bat to his arm. We go for smokes together outside and talk lots. I get released a day later. I walk out the doors of the hospital to the street, then walk back to the hospital doors, then back to the street, then back to the doors. I do this for a good half hour. I am stunned. I feel like I just don't know what to do. I know I must get to my dog, but I don't know how. I get a cab and explain to the cabbie what's up and ask him to take me to my sister's house. At my sister's house, she pays my cab and I fall back to sleep on her couch. I explain that I was in a car accident only. The next day, I go to my mother's house and spend a week on her couch with my dog in the garage. This is it, I think. This just can't go on anymore. Is it possible I have had the sense beaten into me? I see my sister and I see my mother and I see my dog, and I know they are all so worried about me. It hurts me to see them see me. I need to do something.

I call my friend Spok, ask him if he could drive me to drop my dog with a kennel, and if he could drive me to this rehab I heard of in Chertsy, Quebec. Spok is this skinny ex-musician with some sort of faint heart condition, always complaining about some sort of pain somewhere and is always wearing the same pair of subscription sunglasses and some old man hat even though he is only in his thirties. He says yes, and of course, the half ounce of crack I have arranged for the ride might have had something to do with his yes.

Next thing I know, I am riding in his old piece-of-shit Cadillac. We are on the 401, smoking our brains out with crack. Not only was he the youngest driving instructor ever in Canada, or so he says, but to me, he is also one of the worst drivers in the world. Or maybe just when he's high. I don't know, but I am going crazy in his front seat. The bucket seat is worn out with no springs left, and I am wasting all my crack trying to get high with him driving as he is in this shitty ride. I keep asking him to pull over so I can do a toke in peace without the waving of his done suspension. Every time I ask him to stop, he asks me for a toke. I don't give him one, and then he keeps driving. Then I break and do a huge one, give him a small one, and ask him to stop. He asks me for more, and I ask him to pull over. He responds that he will after a big toke, and I get frustrated and do a big one. Usually, at this point, he jerks the car, ruining my toke. At this point, all I want him to do is pull over—not so I can do a toke in peace but so I can murder the motherfucker then take his car and drive it into a fucking wall. I think he knows this, so he doesn't pull over. This goes on for hours till we need gas. Thank God for crack; no, not really.

After eight hours of a hellish ride, we are at last in this town of Cherstey, Quebec, population eight thousand. My ride pulls over into an empty parking lot. I get out of the vehicle, walk a bit. Using my cell phone, I call my intake counselor. I tell her where I am, and she says someone will be where I am in a moment to get me. I walk back to the car, throw my remaining crack at Spok with my pipe, and tell him to pop the trunk. He does. I pull my bags out and strap them all to my body, walk up to the driver's side of the car, and say, "From this moment on, you are dead. All my friends are dead to me, all my family is dead to me, even my dog is dead to me. But if I make it through the days like this, then I might have something again in tomorrow." He drives off. I don't wave; neither does he.

I am standing on a corner in this strange, empty, small Quebec town as I see a minivan approach. I have never been so happy—little did I know I was about to begin the two most horrific weeks of my entire existence. This is another private rehab; I call it Fakehaven.

Now I eat and sleep
through what remains
in an August summer day.

I am showed to my room at Fakehaven; it is neat and tidy. The view from my window is of rolling green hills and trees. This whole place, I get the sense, is surreal. It reminds me of something or somewhere else where I am not right now. I lie on my bed and am asleep instantly. That night, I have the first of my nightmares that would only get worse, saved by some older lady knocking at my door. I have missed breakfast and am late for group, apparently. It is explained to me that I have to be there.

The next three days are a horror of trying to go through the day-to-day motions of this rehab while trying to stay awake. We have class where we read slides, each taking a turn from our desks. Each time my turn comes around, I am found to be sleeping at my desk. The counselor wakes me and asks me to read from the slide projection on the wall. I begin and, before the first few lines, find myself being woken again and again and again. Why won't they just let me sleep? In the basement of the building, we have a group gathering where we all sit with our desks in a big circle as we are supposed to be working on our workbooks. I fall asleep. The other rehab people walk up to me and drop their books on my desk by my sleeping head. I don't jump but just look up stunned; I put my head back down and fall right back to sleep. Our days are a mix of these sorts of classes and outside time where we are supervised like children on recess. Each night is pure terror as I have more and more recurring nightmares.

After around ten days, I am at breakfast and see the last glass of orange juice go to the person in line in front of me. I leave my tray on the line, walk out of the cafeteria, and approach security in their office. "We are out of orange juice," some fat woman in tight bash pants and a uniform blue button-down shirt looks up at me from her desk.

I add, "You best be sending someone to the store."

She just looks at me with no expression. I go back into the cafeteria and grab my tray and sit at a table and begin eating my runny eggs. The food in jail was better than this. I stop eating and just stare at the whole room blankly for about three minutes. I get back up and walk back to the security office. "Well did someone go to get some juice?"

The lady just looks again at me in the same stunned way, like I may be in the room in front of her or maybe she just heard a noise—no difference in how she warrants her glance. I walk out of the office; I am trembling.

I am back in the cafeteria. I walk into the kitchen. I am told that I should not be in there by some kitchen staff person. I walk out back into the cafeteria; the staff guy follows me. I get to where my tray is; he is standing about three feet behind me. I pick up my tray and whip it all—eggs and all, the whole assortment—at him. I now have the attention of everyone in the cafeteria. I wonder if that fat security bitch is looking up again at her desk now, all dumb still. "I want some fuckin' orange juice in the morning with my shitty eggs!" I shout. "Is that too much to fucking ask?" My fellow ripped-off rehab brothers and sisters are cheering. "Twenty-eight grand, and I am going to have water with my breakfast. I don't fucking think so."

I walk out of the cafeteria, outside to our little recess area, and light a cigarette. Two security fucks have followed me outside and are just staring at me from around fifteen feet away. They are giving me mean, hateful looks but say nothing. I walk by them back inside to where the payphones are. I try calling someone, but the person isn't home. I snap! I pick up a chair by the payphones, raise it up high above my head, and crash it down to the ground. The chair breaks into what seems to be a hundred wooden pieces. I walk back to the dumb fat security bitch and tell her I am out of here. She smiles. "No refund policy." I am now up in my room and throwing all I can into a little bag, since they took my travel bags when I arrived. Some older French-speaking man comes into my room and sees me trying to pack. "We call the cops," he says to me.

Within three minutes, all I have is smokes in hand and some little bag. I am walking down some road in the middle of fucking nowhere. After about ten minutes, I see a familiar face in a minivan pull up to me; the man has all my things already packed up in the backseat. I can see how this rehab operates—it is a cash grab with a no-refund policy—and they just made twenty-eight thousand dollars off of me for a ten-day stay. I am in the minivan. The man is driving me to the bus station in Montreal, and I am wondering in my rage: where did all this begin in my life? And I am thinking back to my adolescent youth of drinking, then pot, then rails of coke at high school parties at age sixteen. Regardless of all that drug education in high school, who is really going to convince a healthy young teenage male that he, in fact, is not invincible? That the first time with drugs is too many times? Crack wasn't even real to me the first time I smoked it, although it was there smoking on my pop can pipe. It was not what I was warned about; it did not even get me high. The first time I did smoke crack was to impress some girl who I liked. She wanted to smoke it, and impressing her overpowered any other reality. I did not even care for the drugs, but after I tasted and tasted and tasted again, I was lost, and even that girl slipped from my reality and all that was left to hold on to was the taste. That taste became and became until anything I ever wanted was made into that taste. I think back to when, at twenty-two, I was living with my buddy Carlo. And Carlo is a story of his own—an urban legend of a fuckup from the drug world of Hamilton, Ontario.

Fallen angels fighting past in present—
rehashing, reliving wounds of past wars
millenniums old.
We have been side by side for lifetimes now,
but each moment is like no others existed.
We are dumb and blind.
So powerful. So destroyed.

So I am sitting on the couch of Carlo's and my apartment on the top floor (seventeenth) of the El Matador on Fennel Street in Hamilton, Ontario. The year is 1995, and we are stoned out of our minds. There is barely any furniture. I am supposed to be in Kingston, Ontario, attending university, but I prefer hanging out in Hamilton—getting high, chilling with these dealers, being a driver for fun.

They call me "zoner" mostly because I am zoned out most of the time. In fact, catch me on a good night and I am on at least five or six different drugs: alcohol, pot, speed, coke, ecstasy, and acid at least. Add some crack blasts, home-cook freebase the occasional mushrooms, and you don't get much conversation out of me. The occasional "yes please" if you ask me if I want a blast, and the occasional "shit, was that a red light?"

We are in Carlo's bedroom, completely railed out, and he is looking at the bag of coke that is not his. He punches the wall, breaking it, and smashes some of the dry-wall fine and adds it to the bag. Shit, I think, that's going to sting someone's nose. It is this type of fucked-up behavior that in the end gets Carlo killed.

Carlo is a clunker, but fun as hell to hang out with. They say when he is walking down the hall toward the apartment door, you can hear him coming from the sound of his joints snapping. Others say he can light a Bic lighter with his toes and hit his pipe using his foot; I never saw this. I don't know how it is that Carlo and I get along, but we do, and we have fun driving other people's drugs around town for them. Each day begins with a drive through Tim Horten's window. This doesn't mean we have slept, and most of the time, we don't sleep, taking turns with a cloth over our heads on top of a boiling pot of water trying to clear our nasal passages so we can snort some more shit. We eventually end up just doing tokes of freebase all the time, but this fucks us up a lot and slows down the deliveries. Total heat scores we are walking into apartment buildings at four in the morning with triple-beam scales in our bags and pockets full of dope.

I remember talking with Carlo and setting him free as my friend, as decided at one point I could not get so involved with the circles he was wedding himself with. I was lucky to be Italian and forewarned by my mother of certain individuals to stay away from. Maybe it was the spirit of my father that guided me away because I know I was not really that smart to make such a smart move. But I told Carlo I had to cut him off as a friend when he went to work for some old names I knew in the North End of Hamilton.

I remember visiting him two years later. He thought he was doing well, as he was running his own crack house. But it was not his own; he just sat at the kitchen table for someone else, two guns in the drawer and one always loaded in his hand. He was paranoid, to say the least. I did no drugs with him that night, uncomfortable in that part of the city. So I left and saw him again once more when he visited me while I stayed with a Jamaican friend on the West Side. My buddy told me Carlo's partner was Crooked-Eye Vin, and Vin was in jail, and Carlo had partied away everything and was using up all the credit the two had together with the triads. In 2006, I was partying with some chick who told me she just learnt her old buddy Carlo had just been killed in Ottawa. I found out it was my Carlo, and the story was he was killed, shot in the face to ensure a closed casket for the mother, sending a message even to his family. This is what happens when you can't pay a drug debt. Two years later, I hear Crooked-Eye Vin hung himself. He was always thinking of the devil; now he is with him. Or maybe that last act was a rebellion, a last ditch hopeless assault against Satan himself that was in him.

These are not the only two I know who lost themselves completely in their subscription to addiction. There is also Bate, found overdosed with a needle in a hotel room in Niagara Falls. There is also JonJon, dropped dead from a lethal mix in a crack house in Hamilton. Also, "Ma," the old lady on Rebecca Street who was given someone's methadone to drink. "Uncs," the old man who used to let us take refuge in his apartment, found beaten to death some Sunday morning on the sidewalk of Barton Street. Also "Uncle Lar," my street uncle who died of a blood infection because he was too busy getting high than to go to a hospital. His kids took the government money for the funeral and spent it on crack, leaving their dad's body unclaimed in the morgue. Old man Das, whose clean and prosperous middle-class son had to come to his dad's apartment after his death to find it all looted and full of sleeping crackheads. And Dor, who after being diagnosed with cancer decided to rot away with a pipe in her mouth rather than do the hospital.

There is no glory or fond memories left behind to your family or friends when you die a drug fiend, as they have to come and scrape your name off the streets and the pipe from your dead hand. Probably, they will bury you upside down in your coffin so you can see the devil approach when he comes for your soul. For the choice to use drugs is a choice to do wrong. It is destruction of one's self and, in this, destruction of God himself. When I was a child, Jesus was my best friend. Now when I think of him, there is only numbness and confusion. Sometimes when coming down from my high, I try to pray to ease the pain but stop quickly, knowing the traitor I am.

Dear God, will you take me back now that my money and drugs are done so that I can only leave you again later? I keep my days with the devil and his minions—they are my street family, and when we are not busy getting happily high, we will hurt each other for nothing. Just blow a load of hate and malice into the face of each other's existence. We love to see each other have to want. Enjoy the power of our drugs in our pockets and pipes: the power it means over a fellow craving addict. Before long, one can have the other stripped and dogfucked, quite literally for the amusement of haters. Shadow has had his doggie dick sucked many times by jonesing crack whores.

Now let's see. I have no hope, no God, no nothing except five different dealer's numbers and a place to get high, looking for dope and a bitch and a quiet spot for my dog. There is no *me*, just the want of crack.

Waiting to Die
On a Sunday Afternoon

I am with Fats in our spot on Emerald Street in Hamilton. Fats does not smoke crack, but he is a dealer and, at that moment, of course, my best friend. His girlfriend Stace is a complete schizophrenic, ruining my buzz usually. Stace's problems started after she was apparently run over by her previous boyfriend—twice. Apparently, after running her over, he reversed over her a second time. She wants me to listen to the phone; she says she hears people talking about her just under the dial tone. Yes, she is crazy.

Shadow is in the backyard, chilling, and I am blowing my mind away with tokes, and Fats yells at me from the other room to check the window. I look outside and see at least three cop cars with another car pulled over. They are arresting around four people outside our house, all crackheads whom I know, but our spot is secret and no one knows we are in this house, thank God. One of the crackers jumps up from a lying position and begins running to escape the police. Of all backyards to run through, she picks ours. Now I am at the back window, staring at cops everywhere. They recognize Shadow; now they are looking for me probably. I jump on the bed Fats is lying on; he pulls out four ounces of crack and is holding the bags in his hands. We can hear cop radios outside and cops talking through our window. Fats and I both fall asleep, literally hiding under the sheets.

I wake and it is the next morning, and Stace is in the kitchen. I go in to see what she's up to; she is plugging all the drains of all the sinks in the house with every tap running. She looks at me and gives me a sinister sneer. "So you guys want to do me in. I'll fix you two, you're both going to die." I

90

look in the sink and see in every sink in the house there is some mixture of cleaning liquids and powders. As they mix with the water, strong vapors are emitting everywhere. I run to Fats's room to wake him up; it's not easy to wake this guy up.

"Wake the fuck up! She is gassing the place, we got to get out!" I scream. Fats, waking and fumbling with four bags of crack, shoves them in his pocket and rolls himself out of the bed with a swaying motion. He walks into the living room where Stace is now smashing everything she can find. Unfortunately for her, there is not much stuff to smash. Fats grabs her and knocks her out with a smack. Next thing me, Shadow, Fats, and some bleeding pscho knocked-out bitch are all squeezed in a little Nissan, and we are driving. I am told to go up to a certain house on the edge of town. As I am driving, I am nodding off, and Fats keeps me awake while I am driving by continuously twisting my ear. We get to our destination. I am in buddy's washroom, and I stare at my ear for a good ten minutes, wondering if it will ever look the same. Soon forgotten with a toke.

A Bloody Meal

So I am with Fats, and we are at Stan-O's mother's house on the edge of the city. His mother is at her cottage. Stan-O is some sixty-something-year-old retired carpenter guy who lives with his ninety-something mother. When this guy does a toke, he freezes still for like a good ten to fifteen minutes; it is quite something to see. We are in his lavish basement, and he is stuck from a toke. I look at Fats and say that I am going to raid the kitchen.

I enjoy cooking and cannot remember the last time we all ate an actual meal, so the dog and I are half in the fridge sniffing it out. This kitchen is stocked; I mean it. Nice tomatoes, Asiago cheese: all mine and Shadow's favorites! In less than hour, I have cooked up three different types of pasta each with different sauces, fried chicken, and killed his ma's blueberry pie. Shadow and I find a couch and fall asleep almost instantly. The kitchen is a disaster—almost every plate and pot dirty, fridge empty. But we are full, and Fats is fed, and all is good to us. But where is Stan-O? He is frozen in the basement at the bottom of the stairs, looking up at the shadows from trees through the front window. Hours go by.

So I am woken by Shadow growling on the couch beside me. My eyes open, and I see six feet away from me Stan-O there. "Youuuuu, youuuuuuu, youuuuuuuu!" He is six feet away, but the tip of his pointing finger is only about three feet away from me. He seems to be stuck on the word *you* now. It dawns on me that we ate all his food supply while his mommy was away, and to boot, we left quite the disaster in his kitchen. Either those two things, or maybe he had just done all his crack. "My kitchen, youuuuuuuu!" Nah, it's the kitchen thing.

I get up just as Fats comes in the room. I am putting a leash on Shadow and getting ready to go. Stan-O backs up a bit and then does a short charge at me, smoke almost coming out his ears, but he stops just a few feet away and then just repeats, "Youuuuu!" He repeats this a few times. Shadow is beginning to get upset; so am I.

"Listen, you fuck!" I scream "I will help you clean your fucking kitchen, just calm the fuck down!" Now the guy is just vibrating upset; I guess I am not allowed to speak in his house either. "Now if you don't get out of my face, I am really going to snap on your gray-haired ass, understand? So FUCK OFF!" I end in a scream. He charges again, and Shadow barks. Stan-O has probably moved a foot, and I already have one of his mom's antique chairs in the air flying toward him. Fats somehow suddenly appears in the middle and puts out his arm to block Stan-O from the chair; the chair hits Fats's arm and breaks clean in two. The bottom half goes to the ground, but the top half still has its flight intact and whims just a bit upward and bounces off Stan-O's head.

Stan-O staggers; his hands are over his head. He removes his hands and holds the palms out to me; they are pure red. "Youuuuu, youuuuu cut me, yoouuuuu've made me bleed." Before they even probably heard me say nothing, Shadow and I are out the front door and then gone. Fucking crazy crackhead, I think to myself.

It's about thirty minutes later, and I am back in the city at one of Dan's spots. I walk in the door, and he throws me a fifty piece. I leave Shadow with him and go sit upstairs and do a few big blasts. About ten minutes and someone downstairs needs a ride. I have my ride ready, and it is quite a nice ride, less the fact that the windows don't go up. So if it starts to rain, you are fucked. This is not a problem right now. Shadow and I, with some Jamaican dude, are driving. Destination: Leamington, Ontario.

Countless night trips
traveling corridors of darkness—
lights do nothing
but reveal more darkness.
Yellow lane markings the only sign
that man once was here.

I wake in my little red Volkswagen Jetta, engine running. I am sleeping behind the wheel; beside me is Sel, snoring. Shadow as well is out cold in the backseat. We are all sitting in the car, which is sitting on the right lane of the number 8 highway somewhere between Hamilton and Caledonia. It is around four or five in the morning. I guess I fell asleep while driving; the car must have rolled to a stop.

I wake Sel; the dog wakes too. "Shit, where the fuck are we?" Sel grunts.

"Fuck, man," I say, hitting the gas to start moving. I am nodding at the wheel again. Sel is already back to sleep; Shadow is back out as well. I see some sign of civilization and turn into a Tim Horton's. Next I remember waking again behind the wheel. Again, the car is running; this time, headlights of a cop car behind us. I slowly hit the gas and begin through the drive-through; the cop car just stays where it was behind us. Maybe they are sleeping too.

So we finally get to where we were going in Caledonia, some fat chick's apartment who has money for Sel. Now we are en route back to Hamilton. This way it is all downhill, so if I fall asleep, there will be no rolling to a stop. I scream the whole way back—so long as I am screaming, it is impossible to sleep. If I stop screaming for more than three seconds, I immediately begin to nod. Both Shadow and Sel think I am nuts.

We arrive back to our spot in Hamilton on Duke Street and file into our basement apartment. We have already picked up our crack; Shadow stays out in the car. We are exhausted, and even with crack, Sel falls asleep on the couch. I am half awake on the other couch. I have been given some crack to sit with and smoke and so to keep watch. Kimly comes in the apartment all ecstatic because she has a date lined up with some dude in five minutes. This dude is gonna pay one hundred bucks to get fucked, and in more ways than one. She runs back out of the apartment and then reappears with some poor, but rich, son of a cunt, and he gets shuffled into the bedroom down the hall. Kimly goes in the kitchen; she is pulling out candles for the room. She goes back into the bedroom. I make sure the apartment door is locked and sit back down. I do a toke and, still the same, nod off.

I think maybe not more than ten or fifteen minutes and I wake to the apartment door slamming shut. I am coming to but am confused because I can only see from the ground up around five feet, and the rest of the apartment is thick gray smoke. Kimly is screaming, "Fire! Fire! And all she does is run down the short hallway and then run back the same way repeatedly, all stupid, waving her hands around. Shit, I think. I go into the hallway, and the smoke is worse. I look into the bedroom and see all the drapes on fire, and the flames are catching to the ceiling. I run back to Sel.

"Wake up, Dread!" I scream. When this guy sleeps, he is almost impossible to wake. I am shaking him violently. "Wake the fuck up! The whole place is on fire!" Something registers in his mind in his distant reality, and *bamm* he is up. He shoots up off the couch and standing straight up, and I can't see his head because it is in the smoke. I see one hand go in one spot to check his money; another hand checks his dope. All is good, and his hand grabs my wrist and I hear a "Let's go, man. Shit, fuck, stupid scunt bloodclut! What she do this time?" It's less than a minute, and Sel and I are walking quickly out the building's back parking lot to Shadow in the car. It is morning, like about 5 or 6 a.m. Everything seems so still and quiet, so stark a change from the interior of the apartment. It would be impossible to know that apartment was on fire unless you looked right into the basement window.

Moments later, Sel and I are around ten blocks away sitting in a Tim Horten's. The whole city is still quiet as you could ever imagine; then, suddenly, it begins. Piercing through the serene quiet of the morning, suddenly a siren starts, then a second one flies through the air behind the first. Within another twenty seconds, the city sounds full of sirens from every direction. Someone waking in their bed to this would probably think the whole city was ablaze. Little would they know it was just a basement crack apartment that ignited, just as little do they let themselves see it. It is just these drugs that are igniting society itself on consuming itself.

And now it seems
like it is all the same—
faces no longer different,
each of us spilling over into each other in likeness.
In each town, there is one of us the same:
one of me, one of you.
And if I see you, I could not tell from when or where
'cause there it would be so many first times encountering.
And if you see your double, you die.

From one city to the next town to another city, the scene of drugs, especially crack cocaine, is very much the same. Characterized with madness and insanity, depravity and perverseness yet very much always occurring in similar patterns. We may be drug addicts or depraved souls, but we are still people all the same. And very much, we carry resemblance from one to another, in many towns of different folks, the people I have smoked crack with, fought with, fucked with, all share so much of each other. It is uncanny. I am in Leamington; the dog and I have a room at the Days Inn, and we have been partying with crack hoes in this room for several days, rarely leaving. This is the strangest motel room I have ever smoked in. The door to the motel room is to the parking lot, which is to the rear of the building. The back of the motel room has a sliding glass door that goes out to a huge indoor pool shared by all—filled with families swimming, it seems, all day and night. Thank God for drapes, because what is going on in my motel room is not for the fainthearted, or pretty much any one with a heart.

At all times, there is a police car parked in the lot, and when I leave to go to the front of the motel, he follows me. When I return back to my room door from the front of the motel room, he follows me the same. Everywhere I go in town, he follows and pulls me over around three times a day. The first time he pulled me and Shadow, he threatened to shoot Shadow for his barking. The cops in this town remind of mall security guys, but they have guns. Apparently, Leamington is like the only town outside of Windsor in that area of Southwestern Ontario that has its own police force; the rest have provincial police. For such a small town, this town's police department is huge, the reason being . . .

It is an August month, and the days don't consist much for Shadow and me. We hang out mostly in our room, sometimes at some cracker's apartment, sometimes just driving aimlessly while smoking. The jeep windows don't go up. I had dropped a forty piece under the window switch and made the mistake of telling another smoker, left her in the car with Shadow and came back to find all the window buttons popped out and half the inside door panel pulled off. Next it started raining, and the whole electrical shorted out. So when we drive and it starts to rain, often we have to change direction and just drive with the rain till it stops just to avoid getting drenched. I am constantly at the money mart to get money transfers for cash to buy dope, and I am one afternoon there about to get my money. And just a moment before I have it in hand, the transfer is frozen. I freak out. I go to leave and slam the door of the money mart. The whole door's glass shatters; this is not good. I look at the clerk; she is staring at the glass as it slowly cracks away from where it was. There is just a long steady sound of crackling glass; it seems to go on for minutes. I tell the lady I will be back in a moment. I jump in my jeep, and I am gone.

I have just enough gas to make it to the next money mart that is in Windsor. As I am getting my transfer, cops show up in the parking lot, question me, and then let me go. Ten minutes later, driving in the city, I am pulled over by three cruisers. They ask me to remove Shadow from the vehicle. It seems Shadow had stashed and was sitting on top of three pipes he had found. The cops tell me I am not going to jail but am to get right back in my jeep, get on the highway, and never come back to Windsor. They know who I am somehow, about my motel room in Leamington, and that I am not going to carry on my party in Windsor. In three hours, I am back in Hamilton at Dan's house.

Old man we called Pa,
he killed himself with the car running
in the garage of the house with shut-off hydro.
I know he wore lime-green underwear
'cause he lent me a pair.

So it is Hamilton the East Side, and we are snug in a house full of candles—hydro bill too high to pay. When we started hanging and smoking at Pa's, the house was orderly and with power, furniture, cupboards with food, and with loving relatives who would call the phone in concern for their wavering old man dad. By the time we were done, Pa was dead, the house dark and empty just with Shadow's shit all through the basement, and we would have moved on to infiltrate the houses of his two sons, both put on the pipe by their daddy's nice little crack-whore lady friend.

I have been awake for over six days, and Fats is forcing me to sleep by cutting me off the dope. I am on the couch in the front room of the house again, flip-flopping like a fish, tisic as hell. I kind of come to screaming from the kitchen; it is an open concept house, so the only thing that makes the kitchen not the front room is the ending of rug and beginning of tile and cupboards. So screaming, ya its 'Din' screaming, "Ah my fucking god, he's not breathing! Check his heart, I think he's fucking dead!"

The whole house vibrates as Fats runs to the kitchen. I can hear them calling 911. I stretch up off the couch for the moment and look in the kitchen to see old man Pa lying flat on the ground. Must have been a big toke; he does that often. I think he is trying to kill himself; it's not to get high anymore.

There is a mad scrambling to clean up all the paraphernalia in the house, as overdose calls are usually one ambulance, one fire truck, and yes, usually one police unit. I am back to flopping around on the couch as I see circling lights outside. Fats opens the front door to the paramedics.

The paramedics circle their eyes, and next thing I feel are hands on me. What the fuck? I think to myself. I focus to see two paramedics standing over me. They are staring at me in disbelief. I am on my back on the couch but have my legs straight up in the air and spinning them like I am riding a bicycle. I hear Fats's voice from behind the paramedics, "Not him, you doughnuts, in the kitchen."

"Holy shit," one utters as they turn to see some dead-looking old man on the floor.

Surprisingly, Pa is woken back to life by the paramedics, and he refuses to go to the hospital with them. He probably didn't want them to see his brown-smudged shit-stained lime-green underwear. The paramedics leave reluctantly back out the front door. That's right. No, I am staying here on the couch too, I think to myself. I have to be careful; I am wearing one of Pa's lime-green underwear too.

In the end of today
I see it all just as memories
I put them down, put them aside
Load my pipe
Hit it
And drive and drive and drive
More and more and more

I t is about one month later. I have been clean for three weeks after a brief stint in a detoxification center. I am back in Hamilton looking to score. I have a wad of cash, a fresh ready-made pipe, Shadow in the backseat, and a jeep filled with supplies for a weeklong road trip in any direction. Just need some dope to complete my disaster.

One morning I will awake and think of crack and decide not, but until then, I am just as I appear: and that is a crackhead. Until then I am imprisoned to myself and a hopeless pursuit of desire that can never be fulfilled. I am not my own, only what I crave, and if crack were truly that then maybe at one point the craving would stop. It is not that I truly crave the drug; it is the drug that is a false solution to a false problem. A wanting for a want that really does not exist. This whole thing is just a simple confusion that I cannot find myself out of.

I have found my dealer, got my dope, and I pull over and hit my first toke in some time, and holy shit, I begin driving aimlessly for hours and hours and hours.

Morning turns to noon to evening to night; my drive is a series of endless puffs and a growing paranoia of all the cars on the road that I see. From the city to the country through cities through country again. It is now like ten at night, and I pass a gas station and figure the next one, I better stop. I keep driving; the gas light is on. I turn to go back to the gas station I passed, get to it, and it is closed. I have only one option: keep driving till I hit Owen Sound. It is like thirty kilometers away, and I doubt I can reach it. It's not that I don't have money, it was just I have been too fucked up to stop. But now I have no choice as the engine revs disappear, indicating I am at last out of gas. The jeep drifts to the side of the highway. It is eleven o'clock; it is eleven kilometers from the next town. Do you know where your children are?

Three hours later I have gas, and Shadow and I get a room at a Comfort Inn. You could call us Comfort Inn junkies, them being pet friendly and all.

So morning comes, and I wake and I am not my own. So I had been some time without using, and yesterday's escapade was like an alien invasion. I mean this morning I feel the drugs in me still but not their high effect—they are like invaders in me, and all they want is more of their kind in me till there is nothing left of me. That's kind of how drugs are: they speak your mind for you, and next thing you know, you have no mind left. One hour and the dog and I are speeding back toward Hamilton for more dope. Both the dog and I are both passengers on this trip—it is yesterday's trip instead being the driver, trying to maintain itself into today. It is not long, and I have scored more dope now driving north east. I have gotten like seven grams of crack, and subconsciously, I am fighting the drug alien in me. Trying to trick it, that if I run out of drugs far enough away from more, I may have enough of a delay in picking up again to gain back control. Problem is I get so high driving I just do circles, never really getting any farther away from Hamilton.

In the desert of my desertion,
in my destruction of this world and all it contains—
I have even lost what there is to destroy.
There is nothing left to destroy.
All is already destroyed, laid to waste, waiting for collection.
In the disarray of my soul, I have found a paved highway
lighted with brightness of delusional pursuits of wants and
desires that have
led me to a metropolis of sin: a city.
Parks of unkempt people living in tents and dirty blankets,
getting high ignoring and chasing some fucked-up dreams.

So I thought Hamilton was bad: enter Montreal. I am about an hour north of this city. I am down to resin and I am not willing to give in to sleep, so I turn around on the highway and head into this Montreal. Within two hours, I have scored my crack and have run in with a new circus crowd.

So the dog and I are in the park downtown, next to the bus station. There in the plain openness of a summer's afternoon, we smoke our pipes with our fellow crackers in the midst of this seemingly buzzing metropolis. From one park to another we move, now toward the water, and here in this park are actual tents pitched. These tents are crackhead homes, occupancy two or three—often, if sounds are coming from inside, these means pipes are full; if silent, most likely dead bodies are sleeping.

It is amongst these that I find my guide Bob, an older Jamaican gentleman who always knows where to take me for the best dope at the moment to score. So it's a blast, quite literally, with Bob driving around the city aimlessly for days at a time, looking for a place to park to do a toke, then seconds later driving off again. Actually it is quite mad, and eventually, I find out that Bob himself goes quite mad. So we have not seen each other for a day or two, and I run into him and he tells me how a whole bunch—him and some others—were getting arrested, and the cops had some guy just walking by hit Bob in the head. This guy did this and a bit more, and the next time Bob did a toke around me, he had quite a strange reaction. You could say that when Bob got hit that day he did lose his marbles.

So he does a toke and just lies back in the passenger seat of the jeep, and he starts talking so softly. I say "what?" but then I realize Bob is talking to himself.

So we are in the jeep; it is parked, and bob is reclined in the seat next to me. I am trying to get the pipe from Bob so I can do a toke, and every time I reach for it, he goes kind of nuts. "Shish, shish, sh, sh," he goes frantically, like someone is coming. Then as I am looking around, he hits the pipe again.

"Two woman," he says.

I say, "What?"

"There is a woman on both sides of the jeep."

I look around; there is no one.

"Ya, baby," he says, talking to some imaginary person. He just sits reclined in the jeep, talking dirty to no one through the jeep window.

"Bob, snap the fuck out of it."

He springs up in the seat, Shadow barks at him, then again he bounces himself against the dashboard. Shadow barks again. He bounces against the door, half goes out the window. Shadow barks a third time, and Bob has now jumped out the open window of the jeep. Pipe in hand, he is running away down an alley. Shadow and I never see Bob again.

So I am driving with Shadow and we run into another figure we know. His nickname is Joka, and he is some Latino lad. We go score and drive around smoking. It's Sunday afternoon, and I am out of money. I park the jeep, and it becomes our room for the night. Shadow and I sleep quite comfortably parked on side streets in the city. In the morning, Joka returns with a bundle of cash and some dope. He makes money as a gay prostitute in some park. We assume our driving aimlessly—in Montreal downtown, one could just drive in circles constantly and, it seems, never stick out. There is an endless stream of Cree Indian crackhead girls, God only knows how old—actually, their family must know, but you just can't find them. It is not long and I am out of gas and money and dope and just with dog food. Shadow, Joka, and I drift into a parking spot on some street near McGill University. I plan to camp here again till morning. Joka takes off to go do his thing, Shadow is in the backseat dining, and I break and begin feasting on an easy-open can of Pedigree Pal with him. I use a dog biscuit as a spoon; when done, I can eat the biscuit. This dog food is not bad at all. Joka never returns. I guess even a gay prostitute crackhead has his standards to the company he keeps, and apparently, I have sunk below such standards, living comfortably in my car with my dog off of dog food and people's garden hoses.

So the next day I am walking down St. Catherine's Street from the bank where I just received some money, and I meet up with this fat Peruvian guy; let's call him Perv. He is tisic as a motherfucker and is actually bouncing off walls to people on the sidewalk then back off the walls of buildings as he walks. Perv recognizes me from one of the parks and whistles for me to meet him down the street. Next thing I know, Perv, Shadow, and I are driving about the city; he sees a cracker and yells at me to pull over. I do. He services the clients, then I drive. Like this for a few hours, finally he directs me to an apartment. I tell him I will meet him in there in fifteen minutes. He goes ahead. Shadow and I go for a walk and snack on some biscuits then go to meet Perv in the same crack slum apartment.

The door is open, and I push it open all the way. Some forty- or fifty-old-something redhead lady meets me at the door. She is covered in like inch-big red bumps and spots, some actually oozing. She says she was attacked by bees; a whole hive apparently emerged from nowhere from a hole in her floor the night before. Wow. I sit on a chair, and Perv throws me a toke. I hit my pipe and begin looking around anxiously, wondering in my buzz where the fuck the bees are at.

I am starting to get tired—that's an understatement. It has been a week, and maybe I have slept a total of ten hours this week. I have not showered and have been living on a diet of dog food and chocolate bars. I am driving just east of Montreal and figure to myself this must stop. I stop and use the phone. I call my friend Dan back in Hamilton collect. I tell him I need his help. He tells me where he is and that he is waiting for me. It is not long that I am in Montreal one last time to score, so I think. I get about three grams of crack and jump on the highway, hit a gas station to fill up on gas, and go to a McDonald's and begin toking away as I head back to Southern Ontario. I can feel my body degenerating; my muscles are almost gone. I think the only muscle I have left is probably an apple-sized heart. The pain has arrived through my high, and even when I am inhaling my dope, I have shooting spasms of pain through my arms and wrists. It is like if I was not high, I would not even be able to steer.

I am driving as fast as possible to get to Dan's. I finally get there. I park the car, and Shadow and I run into his house. We find he is not there, but his girlfriend says he is just outside Windsor. So I score again locally and am again driving. I am so tired. I begin nodding off to sleep in between tokes. I have my arm out the window and repeatedly am banging it against the side of the jeep to try to stay awake; at the moment, this is working better than the crack to keep me up. Every time my hand hits the outside of the jeep door, there is a shot of pain from my wrist to my shoulder. Sometimes it runs right out to the other side of my body. In the end, after like ten hours of driving, I find where Dan is: in some farmhouse in the middle of nowhere in Southwestern Ontario. There is some dealer there with him, and he throws me like five grams of crack. I sit on the couch and do a toke and then there is darkness.

> Waking from a sleep,
> finding one is still nowhere lost.
> When young, I used to wake from nightmares.
> Now old and addicted, I wake into them.

Often, even when one is exhausted, one can hold on, staying awake somehow amazingly even after days and days of no sleep. Until one is around or back in a safe environment, realizing this, the emergency drive shuts down and sleep instantly takes over. Just seeing my friend, someone who I knew I could trust with myself and Shadow—even after a monster-sized toke, sleep takes over. But this is beyond sleep. Maybe it's half sleep and half death, a closer relative to death than sleep. I am not sleeping. I am shut off, better to say.

I wake to where I was not. I am on a couch. The room is full of light coming in from the windows. There is a bed not far from me and a desk with a computer on it. The rug is shag and it is a cream color, the walls are painted green, and there are two windows. I wonder, maybe I am still sleeping. No, I am awake. Then where am I? I start my mind. Where am I? What time is it? What day is it? It is—no, I cannot remember. Let me try the month. Panic begins to set in. Where is my dog? Complete terror. I try to get up. It takes minutes and minutes, and my mind keeps racing the same questions it can't answer. I begin screaming.

Dan runs into the room. "Robbie, it's okay!"

I am in complete terror; it is like I am awake but mind is off still. I don't even know who I am. Then little things start returning to me one by one. I sit up.

"Wow," Dan says to me. He has never heard someone scream like that before in his life. My lapse has terrified everyone else in the house; they are all fucked on crack also. I get up and begin walking around. I might as well be a nut in a loony bin. I go out on a porch and see Shadow lying under a tree. I sit on the ground beside him, hold him, and begin to cry. I have never been so close to being just a vacuum before in my life. I have no being, just a burnt-out body and mind. I am just a reminder of someone who once lived.

Often when I think back to my years and years of drug use, I tend to only think of the good side. Yeah, as if there was really any. But every time I relapse is because I am focused on just one moment by itself separated from all the preceding and proceeding moments of drug addiction. Now my body is destroyed, and if I don't stop smoking this crack, I feel like I am going to die. It is a Saturday. I walk back into the farmhouse and say to Dan, "Drive me to rehab now. I won't live to Monday at this rate."

We drop my dog in a few hours, and the next day, I am hugging Dan good-bye. Two girls off the street came for the ride. One turns to me and says, "Black Rob, you have had so many chances at cleaning up, most of us never have one chance. If you want to make it so that you deserve this chance, then you must make it this time. Otherwise, you did not deserve any of your chances at all."

I walk into the intake office of the rehab, barely strong enough to carry my own bag. I feel a mess. I had done my last toke not too long ago. I feel like a slobbering maniac unable to stare these sane people in the eye.

Sometimes you got to give something up to truly gain
something back.
Sometimes you need to take a little time to gain some real time
back.
Sometimes you got to go somewhere to get to be where you are
already.

There is me, some goofy balding blond guy from Hamilton as well, some American Bostonian coming off heroin, and another adventurer crackhead just returned from Costa Rica. All of us in rehab and none of us makes it through this journey. Not this time around.

It's just what happens. Not to say the next time it will not be different. It's like everybody has to be at "that" point to make it work for them, and if it is not "that" time, then it's not going to be a success. What it is that makes it that time for you to finally stop using is you, and this is complete honesty and a clear decision and commitment to a new type of life. But it is beyond one's knowing, I think, even for oneself to know. Problem is, most addicts get to the point where they have used for so long that they don't realize it is not about just stopping the drugs, it's about changing how you approach yourself and how you approach the smallest things in life. In general, the same wrong decisions about things other than drugs will lead you right back to drugs again. It really is a question of honesty, but even so with utmost honesty, therein still lies a hidden hurdle—something there that if you refuse to acknowledge it, you fail by tripping over it. A separation is necessary not just from drugs but from that void altogether. How do I do this? Well, at that point, I thought I knew but really did not. I later find out this all requires finding God and then putting him first. Yeah, just like the twelve steps after all.

So I am walking around the halls of this rehab, and I am losing my mind for real. I cannot get over the fact that this is my third return to the same place for help. Each time, I have had no choice but to come back or die. It is destroying me and who I value myself to be, to think that I cannot live on my own without the support of some sort of rehab. It's like I feel I am becoming institutionalized, and this idea itself I take to be as terrifying as drug use itself. Either way, either road I look down, I see nothing positive. When I am alone in my room, I talk to myself as if I am talking to my dog still. And this reminds me of my betrayal to him, and this is a deadening self-inflicted hurt on myself. I get angry. I walk it off. I get angry. I walk it off. I feel I am definitely losing my mind.

So the Bostonian goes home. And I am thinking, knowing it is to go use again. I am in class doing this rehab's version of meditation and I can smell the sin on the staff themselves. It disgusts me. They are self-righteous and wrong, and I cannot get over this. And this, after a few days, gets in the way of what is really important to me. I blow the program. On my way out, I see a woman who works there who was in the program with me some time ago, and she says to me, "Don't think I don't see it on your face what you intend to do." I am enraged by this comment. I mean I have no intention to use; I just cannot handle it at the center I am at. I mean this is my fourth time there, and it is killing me. I call her a cunt and a piece of shit. As I walk out the hallway to leave the center, I hear her laughing at some small joke someone else throws out. She's laughing and all almost in the same breath of speaking to me. What fucking insincerity; all this person cares about is really about herself. Fuck them all, I think to myself. I will do this on my own.

I later find out that the two others who I came in with left as well. At any rehab center the most important thing is the integrity and honesty of its staff; if there is no professionalism, there is no hope in hell for any of the clients. I am and can do it this time. I know I can, and I don't need this fuckin' place to succeed. Not to say all of the people who worked there were all bad. No, but off the mark for a drug rehab maybe.

As far as the staff at that time working at that rehab—well, besides Brad Janes being one of them, also Jewel plus four other staff either piss dirty or admit to using drugs within six months, so my eventual return to drugs put me in a personal wrong. That did not make them right, but I would still go back there, forced by circumstance one more time.

Outside, a war rages in which what is lost is our own family
and friends.
If you cannot see this, you just refuse to recognize—
don't think those lost souls on the street once belonged to a
lover's arm
or a mother's embrace.
It is ourselves we refuse to see who are dying in addiction on
the streets.
If you are not willing to fight for one's own, is it really worth
waking up to?
One's only excuse is that one does not care about their fellow
person.
One day, it could be you or your child on the corner.

So I am doing well, and it's been like four months since I walked out of rehab and started on my own again. It has not been easy, and I feel like I have been ostracized by my supposed friends for not getting clean their way. Oh well, all is well until after New Year's Eve, morning, about 4:30 a.m. I take off in the jeep for Montreal and begin my search down alleys and downtown for some good old-fashioned Quebec crack. It is not long till I am in the parked jeep, pipe loaded, jeep loaded with freaks, and hours have gone by. I hear fireworks; the crowds in the streets are cheering on the New Year. It is the New Year. I look at my pipe and think, fuck it, and I bring in the New Year in the worst way. What a toke. The cheers of people on the street echo away, each moment more distant. They have not gone, but I have moved myself away, put myself back alone without God or anyone, just the countless night faces all different but the same. I wake myself in the mind, body, and intention of an impostor.

I get back to my apartment and lock myself in for days, sedating myself with food, only going outside for moments for Shadow to go the washroom. I am holding on to a thread, holding on to something inside of me that keeps me to the surface but not my head above the water.

My phone rings around the fourth day, and it is the rehab center I departed; they think I am doing well. The gentleman asks if I would like to come in to volunteer a few hours a week. I know that to say yes would be for me to not use again, but inside I am just counting the days till I feel it's safe to return to the crack in the city. I say no. I have forsaken God and now my neighbor. A couple days later, I am back in Montreal. This time I discover Chez B's, a VIP crack house on the East Side. But all over the city of Montreal, just one inch below the surface, drugs are everywhere. I am told by people on the streets that this is happening everywhere in Quebec, that it is the bikers' revenge.

It is in Montreal that I come across, for the first time, an actual crack bar. Yeah, that's right, a crack bar. I go through a door on St. Catherine's Street, up one set of stairs, and I am in a bar with some working girl. And yes, that's right, she just ordered from the waitress a forty piece for me and some screen. Less than a minute later, we are served our crack at the table. I look around and see others at other tables, smoking away at their pipes, waitresses busy appearing then reappearing. Each toke I take, my world darkens, and I am put closer and closer with the anguished and haunted remnants of all dark souls of all times. With each toke, the world slips farther away, and I slowly emerge into an old dark reality filled with silent voices speaking paranoid visions of retribution. Each moment, fear grows, and I cling on to my crack pipe in this cold, lonely, unholy world. This is the same old drug and addiction but seemingly now putting me so far away from something; this new darkness is unreal. It is unfathomable. Like God himself has withdrawn from this world, and everyone knows it and doesn't care, and neither does God.

I left to save my body,
to restore my soul.
Excuse the time,
it wont be long. I love you.
God bless you; I miss you.

My eyes open, and I am sober. I am alone. Shadow is with his breeder some 800 km away. Without him, I fix my bags and get dropped by Dan again, this time the fifth return to this rehab, at Nonsensenon. I approach the door of the building; no one is anywhere. I circle the building to the rear and find someone who works there on the side porch; she radios for security. I go back to the vehicle to say good-bye to Dan; he waves good-bye as I am left with my bags. I am approached by security, some shady-looking ex-rehab patient. "Rob, it's good to see ya."

A week or so goes by where I am kept in a secluded part of the building while I am in withdrawal. The other new arrivals are called fresh starts, meaning it's their first time at the rehab. Me, it's like my fifth return. The fresh starts get all the attention and care. I just pretty much sleep straight through the first few days then begin going for walks then start my push-ups. It's like I respond positively to this lack of attention: this seems to symbolize my whole stay at this rehab this time. I pretty much have no program; I just do what I think is good for me to recover. I ask for the sauna program, and that's it, and about two weeks after arriving, I begin my daily sweat lodge.

I am sitting in the sauna; it's been like twenty-seven days or so now in a row that I have been sweating in this box for about four hours a day. I am up to like twenty-eight hundred milligrams of niacin each morning. And I am reacting to the niacin; my flesh is bright red, burning, and itching everywhere: arms, face, worse in my crotch area. I am upset because I was called for an interview upstairs; this would mean I was going to miss a day in sauna and would then be put back another extra day in this box. I had told them I was done, detoxified—they don't seem to think so. Apparently, I am being taken out of the sauna because of a comment I wrote in my sauna journal about not wanting to exceed a certain level of niacin. They are asking me why I wrote this, if I had received information from someone. I am outraged by the reason of the interview. I mean they call me up for an interview like I was done with the sauna, and now it is seeming like I am on hold. I say to the man conducting the interview, "End of fucking interview. I am going back in the sauna as usual, you're not putting me on hold."

I walk down in the sauna, enter the box after taking my niacin, and I am reacting badly. This tall fat bald guy, another client named Pete, is at the window of my sauna door sticking his tongue out at me, laughing. He's done his sauna; he cheated himself his whole way through it. I fling my water jug at the door and charge after him, and he takes off. I am blurred with rage, so blurred I can't find Pete. I fly back to my dorm room on the second level of the building. I push out my screen window and begin flinging my certificates from my previous time at this rehab out the window. Other clients outside are gathering outside my window on the grass below; they think I am throwing my cheese out the window, but it's only their fuckin' useless certificate papers. I am ready to leave. I am walking out as if to leave, but I am thinking I really have no desire to go. A lady who works there, let's call her C, she walks with me a bit. I calm down, and I go back into the sauna area. I sit on the chair by the desk of the sauna lady and say, "I always did exactly what I was told to do in these fucking programs, and the result has always been the same—me relapsing."

I am in tears. I go back in the sauna box. I am so upset. I meant each time I finished these fucking rehab programs, I was clean and enjoying it, each time with some sort of better hope for my life. But in the end, I always ended up worse off than before. Suddenly, sitting in my sweat, I understood. Doing what they say, what they think—that only gets me so far. It is really no solution. Starting today, I have to do what I know is right for me. No rehab program is a cure, no matter what they say or what they say their success rate is. As long as I rely on them or their programs, it will never work. Completing a rehab program does not cure me. Even if I have been sober for months, the threat will not go away. Even this extreme sauna program will not stop me from craving or wanting drugs again. This addiction is, instead, something that must be overcome by accepting, admitting, and living with it, but not under it. After all, every human is an addict to some extent to something. Some of us just have more dangerous toys.

But what is the threat, and what is the solution? Is addiction just something I have attached myself to? Is this simply a problem of my liking and choosing? Is it as simple as a quiet "no" to myself or me listening to myself? But it's me who leads me to the wrong places all the time; there has to be another something to listen to that is pure in guidance, not corrupt like these fucks. Then I remembered when I was in my jeep years earlier about to relapse and my cell phone vibrated to show me that picture of Jesus, and how I had turned the power off on my cell and it just turned back on to show me the image of Jesus again. I was called by God to the Godless. Me, a fallen casualty who no one cared about. Yes, even me that day—God himself cared enough to actually bend all the laws of the physical universe and actually ring me on my cell phone. Break reality and give me a concrete example of his love. God, at that moment, actually demonstrated my saving was more important than me believing or choosing it myself. God put himself at my feet to be rejected by me, a crackhead. That's how much he loved me so that I might, in the end, truly believe and be saved. And some think they have another solution to addiction. No. For me, it is simply God. I put God first and nothing else; each day beyond has been a steady improvement. It was God who would not let go; he loved me too much. And beyond tears, he empowered me to recognize myself in the faces of billions. It was me alone who he did not forget.

So I finish the sauna program, and that morning, I approach the metal cross with Jesus on it. It is a strange juxtaposition because this rehab program is taken purely from scientology books, and they aren't too big on Jesus of Nazareth, to say the least. I wonder what those Scientologists were thinking, or if they saw me when I prayed at the feet of the statue of Jesus. On that day, I feel I can approach this shrine renewed, and I climb right up to the top, grab hold of the cross, and kiss the white stone feet of Jesus—kiss them cold but still lifelike to the touch of my lips. I turned and looked, and for that moment, understood who he was. I mean who God was, and who I was. I mean who man is. And I was asked by a gentleman who was walking by randomly at the time on his way to work, "This time, will you follow him wherever he goes?"

I startled a blind man with vision,

subdued another's tears with the wet of my own.

Pushed in pain till joy was felt.

Walked for miles to arrive,

releasing captives by untouching the soul.

It is now seven and a half months I have been clean, almost six months out of rehab. I am driving the 401 west to visit my mother and sister—the first time in a long time. My cell phone rings; the number is an old friend's from a previous rehab around two years ago. His name is Jack. He is crying at the end of his rope, he wants all the bullshit to end but cannot fathom how to start. So it is a series of phone calls, and within another two hundred kilometers into my ride, an application to rehab has been put in. Within the morning, it is accepted. Jack has packed his bags and signs his last possession over to his girlfriend. With a one-way ticket to Toronto, he arrives at the airport. I pick him up in my jeep with my dog riding in the backseat. The next morning, the three of us begin our thousand-and-four-kilometer drive, first for Jack to say his good-byes to his parents in Northern Ontario and then to rehab in Quebec. The ride is new to him but not to me. All too familiar, I have been driven this way many times by others to rehab myself—crazy rides full of drugs, liquor, and women. But I think this is Jack's moment, his time that he can make it a success for him. There are no drugs or alcohol on this ride, only good music, good friends, talks of family, and God. I know this is a change for Jack, and it is a change for me.

The first time when God called me on my cell phone, I was sitting with my crack pipe loaded one moment before the moment of relapse. But now when God calls on my cell phone, I answer and am happy to answer. At this moment, my cell phone is on with the ringer volume on full, and I keep awaiting God's call in between perseverance and patience. All this and I recognize this had already echoed in my mind before it all happened, like I was told this all long ago by someone in a dream or when I was young but I forgot. But never did I stop believing in what I forgot or did not know. Nor will I; this is to have faith.

Peace Out

"Peace out." Those were the last words said to me by Jack as he walked by me. I was working that day at the rehab, and he was leaving after just two weeks there. Going back somewhere, I don't know where. He earlier smashed up a payphone in the cafeteria and was promptly suspended. I was working at the center at that time, so I had a view from a distance of this happening slightly just before it all happened.

When I awoke the next morning, I found an email from J saying that the rehab center stank of the devil and so on, discrediting the staff as cowards being and staying clean all through their job. So he did not say this directly of me, but he did say he prayed that I would leave my job there. Why such hostility? What was really going on? Was J just placing blame on the center for his own shortcomings? Was he just wanting an excuse to leave, or was someone—or some people—really pushing his buttons? If I look at when I blew this same program countless times, it was never my intention to leave to go use drugs. There was always some sort of trip up by someone there who caused me to blow. But in my last program, even when tripped, even after I got upset, I still did not care to leave. I, in fact, cared too much for what was I was doing for myself and my world to let anyone else make the difference. And maybe that is the difference for me this time. I mean I put myself so close in my faith with God, I have no need of justification with anything or anyone else. My attitude when at the end of my rope almost is a cruel "fuck 'em all" attitude. No one and nothing changes what and why it is what I am doing.

In the end, I never spoke to J again, and I realized how easily I can be used by another addict in their extremity and how careful lies my integrity

120

and morality in a job such as in a place like a private rehab that has no real outside standards imposed on them. Their success is subjectively defined by themselves, and each staff's stature in life is dependent on a close proximity with the failing addict. Sad to say, take these bright and clean-looking individuals out of this rehab and environment and they are suddenly not so exceptional. And me saying they are clean is as much of a presumption as saying they are closet users.

The days that follow my job at the rehab becomes harder and harder on me emotionally. I know so many clients who relapse after (practically all), and the clients demand from me an answer if this will really help them. The answer is, ultimately, nothing can make them stay clean, only their choice. But in fact, I removed the choice from myself to use, and put it all in my faith in God's will. This is actually kind of like a higher-power solution, closer to the twelve-step answer than the scientologist approach Nonsensenon is using. Maybe the center knows this, and that's why they are suddenly pee-testing me all the time. Or maybe it's just that, factually speaking, they know it is more likely I am using than not based on the fact that I graduated their program.

Time and time again, I encounter what they call "suppression" in my job from the center itself—namely, other staff. This idea of suppression is not unique to scientology, but I believe they borrowed the concept of "jealousy" where it seems first to be expressed in the Bible. The center maintains that suppression causes people to make mistakes, errors, be ill, etc. So if this is the case, I should definitely be removing myself from my job at this rehab. I do, but not simply for this reason. There are also the dreams where I wake hearing what I think to be the actual voice of God telling me to leave my job. Also, the moral and religious dilemma this job creates for me. Also, am I helping these people? I mean, clearly from the results, I am not.

I look at this private rehab and see, regardless of the love I do feel for my bosses and colleagues here, I still see that these are people who empower themselves through other people's weaknesses. They need the addict more than the addict needs them.

People coming off drugs, choosing to end addiction, need a good and lengthy detoxification to put them on the right track. But an extended rehabilitation to teach "rules" or "tools" to live anew by—well, statistically,

I have seen just as many do as well with as without. Ultimately, it is more is it that person's time to change or not? Ultimately up to that person or, as I prefer to say instead, God. I do believe some visits to rehab were necessary on my journey to be clean today, but it was more a lesson—and a painful one, if I may add—of showing me what is not, so I could find out truly for myself what is.

So if at that rehab they are helping these people then how much should the benefit from this action, it seems to me they need those people addicted just as much as those other people need drugs. Its not just a job to them it is their righteousness, and also how they survive in itself. It seems a dangerous totalitarianism, they define themselves as group, and even against their own teaching, they put into the practice the supremacy of the group's survival, and constantly subject the individual, or the definition of what is right or wrong, to the group's cause. I personally am not the type to subject the cost of an Individual so that the group survives, and its ultimate survival depends on weakness in its persons, the staff, and other persons, the clients. So this is a view point and the actions conducted at the rehab are seemingly good, but I question the true intention of the group, to me it seems to be truly and only their own survival. Otherwise why would they be untruthful about things such as their success rate, why would they lie and say to a client they can cure them of something of which it is just as clear they cannot cure as much as the possibility that they can. Why do they think and teach that one must do good to be good, why do they need justification so bad.

I had found my strength and hence was simply no longer any use to them. I conveniently excused myself exited myself from responsibility and was easily no longer noticed except when made a target of doubt. I could and did point out lots of people at this rehab questionable, but it seems their weakness was to alluring to be dealt with appropriately. That is morally, they preferred mold to fester in the corners. What is that smell, oh that smell is no smell, no smell is your smell—your shit and it does stink and its not your farts that give you away its your lies and glass smiles.

Their real target was instead strength. I can smell their fear, and I will not bow down and be weak to survive. No, my Lord is all strong and powerful and he has plans for me to do good, to actually be good rather than evil and just have a good reason so to be without an excuse. So I cannot say and I do know this is not typical of all rehabs, but was of the Nonsensenon in Trois-Rivieres where I was. They all can play dumb, we can all play dumb to the scam, but sooner or later if we play dumb long enough we will turn dumb and lots of people have already been hurt by such stupidity.

Motormouth

Her name is "Motormouth." She talks fast, but that is not where her name came from. A once-beautiful blond girl with blue eyes, she is fine and tempting as long as she does not take her pants off. It does not take long to see the damage that the streets have done to her. Only a bit more than a glimpse and you can see a savage mind, dirty fingers, cuts, bruises, and worse, often tears. But only when the drugs are done. It is cold on the February streets of Montreal, and if she has no date, no money, no dope, she is then forced—sometimes literally thrown—from the crack house. As soon as she has twenty dollars, she is again spending it on more crack. "Sucky sucky if you have forty dollars."

Motormouth would always be asking to try my eyeglasses on; I never let her. I know countless people who have had their eyeglasses stolen while in crack houses. I am ushered from her and shown into a room I am renting for a few hours. On the coffee table on a mirror is several grams of crack and on the couch a beautiful brunette assistant to administer me my drugs, care for my pipe, and other needs. But the radio plays and the song penetrates all—the song "Te Amo" by Laura Branigan—and the words are cutting deep. My high is bled away, and now all I can think about is Shadow waiting for me at home. The only thing real to me now is what I have got myself into the last couple months of smoking crack again, that I may lose my dog if not already. How I have no one really left in my life except one or two grieving family members. I think of God and I know all this is not right, and this song on the radio playing never ends. Although I have a full tray of crack and a busty pipe assistant, I feel tears in my eyes. I know I have to go, get back home as quickly as possible, but what do you do when the devil will not let go of you? Everything is working for me to stay in this fake paradise. In the past, return to sobriety was easy.

It was instead hard to keep getting all the dope and such. But this time around, anything with the drugs actually falls into my hands, and it is instead an exit home that seems impossible to come by. This is beyond a temptation; this is being stuck. I rush out of the room into the hallway. I bump into Motormouth; she begins speaking in French super fast. I cannot understand. Then she speaks some English, "I sucky your . . . I do anything, just forty dollars."

I take my eyeglasses off, hand them to her, and motion her to put them on. Suddenly as she dons them, I see an immediate grace of God penetrate, penetrate all: her, me, the room, the house, for all I know the sun could have just risen over the entire city in the middle of the night. This weathered crack whore now bears the semblance of an angelic child, an angelic child in the wrong place. All of a sudden, she is not what she was; nor does she belong there. She now has the smile of an innocent eight-year-old girl, and then yes, tears appear, and more tears. I guess she can see now. I turn and run out the house, leaving her with my eyeglasses. I am wondering: Why is it so hard for me to stop this madness? Why is it so easy to continue when all I really want is to stop?

A year later—and this a year of being sober—I still carry the persons like Motormouth with me. Others as well I cannot forget; they always return in my mind. It seems it is their memories that are slowly replacing my addiction. In the end, the drug's taste and high fade, but what is with me always are those I saw so lost. Motormouth was nearly blind. With my glasses, she could see, and at that moment, I came to know that something had transpired in my soul. I was no longer blind. Yes, I actually became aware to the fact that what I was seeing was sight, and this seeing was, at that moment, a terrifying realization of where I was and who I was being.

Adrift at sea,

saved by a memory—

Jesus eclipses the sun.

And this burning from inside out—

no quenching.

Soul of ice melting into this ocean of life.

I am around nine months clean, and I have just left my job where I was working at a private rehab. A few days out of this job and I catch some terrible bug, and it is not long till I am on the couch alone in my apartment with fever and aches, only Shadow there with me. One of those nights in my sleep, it is like this sickness reaches its zenith and breaks after a war-torn sleep.

It was being fought in each cell as I slept. From one spot to the next, it seemed God was demanding an answer from me, an absolute answer from me. In a feverish cry against all else except God, each of my body's cells in union and sense proclaimed, screamed "Jesus!"

What did this mean? But I was able to and willing to lose all—myself, my life, my dog, my family, forsake everything, lose it all, even my sobriety—to maintain my belief in one man as God that is Jesus Christ. It seemed the question asked of me in my sleep that night, and hence, my answer. All that doubt inflicted on me by the rehab I was working at; all that dogma that they teach to supposedly help addicts. In it, they attack "some churches," discredit the forgiveness of sins, that confession does not work." The fear I had that if I confronted this, it would affect where I stood in my "drug-free group." That I may have a relapse or something even worse.

What was keeping me clean—them or me or a Christian God or scientology or what? Not who is right or wrong. Simply, did they have a noose on me through my addiction?

So I am as real as Jesus himself, and if Hubbard denies that, then I guess he is saying that I do not exist either. So yes, Mr. Hubbard, thanks for your help, and thank you, private rehab, for your help. But when Jesus was crucified for the sins of humanity, that did include all your sins as well.

So I quit my job at the rehab and then got ill a year ago. I quit my job, yes, at this same rehab and then relapsed a few weeks later. So I view just simply getting sick was a bit of a success. Yes, I am thankful to be human again.

Those at Nonsensenon when I quit a year earlier already had me for dead the same day I left. No, they were wrong; it took me a couple weeks to go back to drugs that time because, just like so many of them, I was using this group—but better to say cult mentality—to stay clean while working there. It's us and them; what we know is different than what they know. We are right; they are wrong. We are a group, but individuals do not equal the group. I mean it seems always individuals who are in question and blame and not the conceived of group. This bullshit is not explicitly doctrine, but it's in all the way the rehab operates. Its hands seemingly all move in some ironic synchronicity that I wish to have nothing to do with. Yes, I would rather smoke crack than be part of that. I can sense its darkness; besides, there was really no difference for me as a drug addict working at a drug rehab, especially that one. I was just on the other side of the same yard. I understand I could, and may have been helping people. But was I? I mean, just being a recovering addict, did that qualify me as a drug rehab staff member, or did the Ron Hubbard training course on misunderstood words qualify me? Or were they even qualified? I mean the scientologist auditors who worked there. What is the success of their graduates? Same as any other rehab, if not worse. What are the success rates of rehabs? Well, it's low, but everyone deserves a second chance. But it is only a chance; it's up to the addict to make the odds in their favor. But to say to an addict when they leave the program that they are no longer an addict to me is wrong. And just because someone pretends to not see what is going on, does not make it not underhanded.

So the last time I attended that rehab as a client, I simply did their sauna program and worked my own recovery in my journal in my room. After six weeks, I excelled on their personality test, set standards of what Hubbard considered to be the unaberrated human, and was certified and graduated. So what was different this time around? For one, my closeness to God. Two, my exposure to the godless darkness I could not escape in the streets of Montreal. I was kind of scared, or rather haunted, into cleaning up. And also, the difference was the eventual severing I did between me and Nonsensenon and the ideas it taught.

Regardless, don't think rehabs are bad. Maybe the worse they are, the better it is for recovery. I was called by God to the godless. Me, a fallen casualty. And while coming out of drugs in that void of a rehab, I discovered what was truly real and important to me: who I was and what that meant to me. But I know today if I would forsake God, I forsake everything. But as long as I stay with God, I have everything that matters anyway.

Could This Be The End?

So I am in my jeep, Shadow in the backseat. I am watching Dan walk away. I have just dropped him off. He is diminishing into the darkness of the night; he does not look back to wave good-bye. I am watching him as he goes. He is limping bad, a result of that night being shot and run over. It's been over a year since then, and I am about ten months clean. Having just visited D for a quiet dinner at Keg Restaurant for his birthday, he says I am his sobriety now. I wonder what he means by this. He is plagued by bad emotion. I would say, consequences of his life chosen. He is far away now, but I can still see him.

Something, someone in me, screams inside of me to chase after him. To say no and just follow him back to my old life—it would be so easy. It would be so easy just to let the drugs decide things again. For a moment, it would be such fun. I hit the jeep into drive and begin my three-hour ride home with Shadow.

I wake in the morning, and I am happy. Happy in my choosing, this morning is my making through the grace of God. Is this a happy ending? Sure feels like it.

There was a time when I was not even acceptable to myself. A time of errors, they were too much for even myself to face. My defeats tore me, grieved me, laid me even more to waste. Put away, rejected by loved ones, sworn at, phones taken off the hook because I would call, police called because it was me at the door. Then, not even I could look at myself. But even then, there was always one who remained waiting. Not because of who I once was or because of who I would be again, but simply because of accepting my weakness for no reason at all to his benefit. His call was a hope in tomorrow, a hope in myself. This was Christ. Now, even today that I am all good and the world takes me back as its own with an open invite, I decide not to remain with it or anyone, not even with myself, but with Christ. I rest in his comfort, and remain safe so long as I choose to dwell with him first before all else. After all, it was him before and after everything and everyone else who never left me. No matter what I chose, he loved me the same. After all, it was him who called me on my cell phone. That I can never forget.

Pain frozen into ice,

and its melting many times flooded my world.

I have dug many oceans and filled them,

and on the only island I dwell.

All this in a lesson learnt.

There is no final victory in or of this world,

only a letting go of one's self

and picking up of God what is good.

This is bigger than me

but, strangely, requires that which is me.

First chance, second chance, third chance, fourth, fifth and so on. We all deserve another chance no matter how many times it all goes wrong. If is one is willing, the war is never lost. Where does that leave you who still use, and where does that put me today, someone who is clean? So decide for yourself what you want for yourself. And if you are not wise enough, life will be your teacher, even if that requires the biggest lesson: death. There are a lot of places in this world where one can go for help, and if one cannot do it alone, then any help is better than no help.

Even the blind can show you the way not to go. What is important is one desires what is better. For me, that is God's will. For someone else, believe what you want as long as what you believe is the truth, because just like the big old good book says, "The truth will set you free."

In the end of it all, it was not my life that I could not bear to lose, but it was God I could not let go of. It was this divine presence that had manifested that I could and no longer ever would forsake. And in the end, I have found freedom. A freeing never ending, wholly delivering.

When I was not even two years old, one day my father did not come home. That day, my mother found me crying, and my stare at her communicated that her husband was dead. Over twenty years later, her common-law husband, my dad for some twenty years, would one Sunday morning just get up and leave.

Not a week later, my older brother, the closest being to my existence, was diagnosed with leukemia. I would watch him fight for over a year. In the end, he died while I watched sitting beside him, a blood clot in the lungs. When a child till I was a teenager, I was abused, molested, and once raped. The pain amplified as I grew into a man. I lost my business, my family—everything but my life. I hid myself in drugs for years and years and years. But in my dark silence there was someone, a calling, and now I have been found. Today I am driven; renewed in spirit. A free man as the night sets, I have faith to carry me through the darkness till morning. I am thankful today for both my blessings and sufferings. As far as drugs go, it is like it is not even my choice not to use anymore. It's like it's all been decided for me now. This is why I say I have been saved, made a free man. This is God's doing.

Afterword

I hope all this sheds some light on the addict, the rehab, and ideas of God; that would mean a lot to Black Rob today. I don't mean to cut anyone, but this is a heartfelt testimony based on the real life of an anonymous person. I can swear this all as truth to every word, based on a true story. So if Black Rob is worth saving to God, so is every lost soul. On the streets today it is not strangers committing crimes and living as addicts and prostitutes, but our own family that we may have forgotten. If God cares who are we not too, and what does caring imply, what does it intend in our lives. Rehabs don't hurt but and may even seem to not help, or help, but some sort of detoxification is a great help. But until we acknowledge the truth of God however you may believe in him and put this truth foremost in our lives, I truly do not think happiness is obtainable, or survival of our world is possible, let alone helping an addict. This is just the voice of one person's experience. One human being, but it brings to testimony a true miracle—so one person can be counted as standing his ground and proclaiming the truth of what he sees. I hope you enjoy this account, *When God Called Me On My Cell Phone.*

Also available by Robert Vincent Piro: *A Place Called Wandering,* a book of poetry.

CPSIA information can be obtained
at www.ICGtesting.com
Printed in the USA
LVOW12s0523291117
557969LV00001B/13/P